GLOUCESTERSHIRE

Edited by Claire Tupholme

First published in Great Britain in 2003 by
YOUNG WRITERS
Remus House,
Coltsfoot Drive,
Peterborough, PE2 9JX
Telephone (01733) 890066

HB ISBN 1 84460 196 X
SB ISBN 1 84460 197 8

FOREWORD

Young Writers was established in 1991 as a foundation for promoting the reading and writing of poetry amongst children and young adults. Today it continues this quest and proceeds to nurture and guide the writing talents of today's youth.

From this year's competition Young Writers is proud to present a showcase of the best poetic talent from across the UK. Each hand-picked poem has been carefully chosen from over 66,000 'Hullabaloo!' entries to be published in this, our eleventh primary school series.

This year in particular we have been wholeheartedly impressed with the quality of entries received. The thought, effort, imagination and hard work put into each poem impressed us all and once again the task of editing was a difficult but enjoyable experience.

We hope you are as pleased as we are with the final selection and that you and your family will continue to be entertained with *Hullabaloo! Gloucestershire* for many years to come.

CONTENTS

Calton Junior School

Sean Rudge	39
Satya Talwar Mouland	40

Charlton Kings Junior School

Joshua Jones	40
Abbie Dawson	41
Jack Howell	41
Abigail Sheridan	42
Jacob Stevens	43
Megan Reid	44
William Palmer	44
Eve Dimery	45
Luke Drinkwater	46
Jacob Tait-Bailey	46
Marko Andjelkovic	47
Warren Cannon	48
Lucy Merry	48
Joseph Scase	49
Lauren Shipley	50
Jack Wickens	50
Mary Woolley	51
Georgina Shill	51
Kate Buckingham & Emma Lawrance	52
Natalie Lewis	53
Daniel Mubarak	54
Amelia Tinton	54
Sasha Jacombs	55
Gabrielle Burge	56

Coalway Junior School

Adam Wood	56
Bethanie Burford	57
Jake Marlowe	57
Edmund Rayner	58
Amy Pearson	59
Hannah Worgan	59
Sophie Giles	60

Jade Davis	60
Layla Dovey	61
Lindsey Fowler	61
Laura Knight	61

Foxmoor School

Jack Bullingham	62
Samuel Thompson	63
Nathan Buckland	64
Candice Francis	65
Joanna Bullingham	66
Sadie McDermott	66
Kyle Yam	67
Jessica Line	67
Sophie Martin	68
Jasmine Ebbrell	68

Hatherop Castle School

Benjamin Curwen	69
Carys Chalklin	69
Harriet Bishop	70
Tom Dyer	70
Rosie Williams	71
Georgia Hind	71
Sophia Mackay	72
Stuart Jones	72
Philip Purry	73
Elizabeth Reavley	73
Adam Gerges	73
Felicity White	74
Samuel Evans	75
Fleur Adderley	75
Dawn Stevenson	76
Timothy Knight	76
Georgina Atherton	77
Harry Chalklin	77
Edward Smith	78
Rosie Poole	78

Claudia Holt	79
Tom Perkins	79
Maddie Forman	80
Arabella Pollock	80
Amy Worsfold	81
Lauren Barnes	81
Clementine D'Arcy Clark	82
Emily Chambers	82
Bryony Logan	83
Catherine Walpole	83
Alexander Davis	84
Elliot Greenwood	84

Ingleside PNEU School

Bryony Smith	85
Emily Blampied	85
Maddy Turner	86
Yasmin Lester-Powell	86
Sophie Jones	87

Leighterton Primary School

Liam Bale	87
Aaron Ryan	87
Olivia Carter	88
Emily Clout	88
Alexandra Reed	89
Helen Jones	89
Hannah Williams	90
Guy Crick	90
Laurence Webb	91
George Rumney-Kenny	91
Beatrix Joyce	92
William Bradley	92

Longden St Mary's CE Primary School

Laura Radley	93
Elizabeth Warner	93
Tom Crutchley	94

Sophie Larner	94
Josh Scrivens	95
Gareth Roberts	96
Joseph Yeates	96
Edward Cooke	97
Jack Martin	97
Eleanor Kirby	98
Cherise Price	98
Grace Woodward	99
Jude Wagstaff	100
Jasmine Quiney	100
Rosanna Sinclair	101

Lydney CE Primary School

James Purvis	101
Amy Biddle	102
Christie-Anne Wayman	102
Gabi Olley	103
Stephanie Wilcox	103
Amelia Challenger	104
Ashleigh Bailey	104

Northleach CE Primary School

Nikita Salmon	105
Jonathan Drinkwater	105
Holly Gardner	106
Tom Hancock	106
Matthew Eames	107
Oliver Krisson	107
James Ager	108
George Dale	108
Lorna Rainey	109
Holly Phipps	109
Michael-Sean Hurst	110
Steve Larner	110
Ben Miles	111
Rebecca Mills	111
Jessica Phillips	112

Rangeworthy CE Primary School

George Mullen	127
Sophie Romain	127
Ruby Williams	128
Evie Guest	128
Hannah Cornford	129
Chloe Hopkins	129
Yasmin Pitman	130
Katherine Powell	130
Kurtis Mastouras	131
Laura Butler	131

St David's School, Moreton-In-Marsh

Daisy Lindlar	132
Carl Hardiman	132
Robyn Thomas	133
Esme Baggott	133
Kieran Evison	134
Danielle Tomes	134
Daniel Greenwood	134
Mohammed Mifthaul Hassan	135
Samantha Jeffrey	135
Lucy Jasinkski	136

St John's CE Primary School, Cheltenham

Alannah James	136
Jessica Morris	137
Shannon Fairclough	138
Jack Davis	139
Lucy Bennett	140
Chloe Teakle	141
Neekhil Nanawala	142
Amber Dangerfield	142
Helen Godding	143
Miranda Howard	144
Hazelanne Abbott	145
Candice Holland	146
Denis Thomas	147

Winchcombe Abbey CE Primary School

The Poems

SON AND MOON

Dear Mum,
    It's lots of fun,
Cos, last week we had our wedding,
A few miles away from Reading,
We wanted a honeymoon packed with cheese,
So we thought of the moon, it's okay if you please?
We wrote a letter to NASA,
The reply was very nice-a
And we were picked up for the moon,
Around the late afternoon.
It was quite a long way,
It took a whole day,
Quite boring I have to say,
So all I could do was sit down and chew
The wine gums I packed yesterday,
But *crash!* We landed at last,
But just a bit too fast.
An alien called Wayne,
Delivered to you in Spain,
Well that's so,
    From your loving son, Moe.

Joe Jenkins (10)

THE GALLOPING

(Based on readings of 'Kidnapped' and 'Windy Nights' by Robert Louis Stevenson and 'The Highwayman' by Alfred Noyes)

He gallops and gallops
On the rugged moor
He flees from the Red Coats
A disfigured man
His face scarred and slashed
Fear possesses his mind
He must escape from the wraths of war
Departing on to the mountains
Where he takes his refuge
The Red Coats closing down on him
Exhaustion ensnares him
He slumbers. He falls. Fatally wounded
Escaping the clutch of death
Relief overwhelms him
Until a deadly shot
Drains all life from his weary body
He takes his last breath
And the game ends.

Nadeem Shad (9)

PAPAYA

Each one is a small planet,
With a desolate plain.
Unlocked it reveals a pebbled beach,
A pink sea of flesh,
So mouth-wateringly good,
With seeds as numerous as stars in the sky.
The tropics in a mouthful.

William Threlfall (9)
Beaudesert Park School

THE DEATH OF THE PAPAYA

The peel, like an old man's wrinkled skin,
Yellow and tender, stretched and thin.
Down comes the knife, with its razor blade,
The sharpest knife ever made.
Pink as a sunset, the juice starts to flood,
Down the blade of the knife, just like blood.
Hung and quartered,
Severely slaughtered.
Little seeds fall out like dark stones,
Spilling from their comfort, their shelter, their homes,
This papaya was stripped from its life,
By a sword? An axe? A single knife.

Bella Haycraft Mee (10)
Beaudesert Park School

DISTANT TRAVELLER

A traveller from a faraway place,
Dark skinned,
Round and wrinkled.
Inside,
You are tender and sweet,
With little seeds playing hide-and-seek,
Beneath oozing fluids, oh so deep.
The taste of your dreams from overseas,
More delicious than honey from bustling bees.

Alice Stuart-Grumbar (10)
Beaudesert Park School

PINEAPPLE DREAMS

The sweet smelling,
Delicious tasting,
Edible prickle.

The luscious bubble mellow
And the dry squelchy yellow,
Transported me,
Somewhere far, far away.

Warm on a beach,
In the middle of nowhere,
Surrounded by exotic trees.

Kitty Treverton Jones (10)
Beaudesert Park School

KIWI

F   ond of this fruit am I,
U   nbelievable centre pattern,
R   aindrops being spat in every direction,
R   unning bullets from a gun,
Y   um, yum, yum!

F   ond of this fruit am I,
R   ough outside but a soft middle,
U   nborn fruit trees inside the black drops,
I   nside grass encased in bark,
T   ake off to a tropical island.

Rose Somerset (10)
Beaudesert Park School

PAPAYA WORLD

The knife falls down,
Cutting into the forests and deserts,
With its only protection falling about it,
The papaya succumbs to the knife's cruel blade,
Splitting - exposed - for the world to see.

Inside a chasm of huge spheres,
Each orb teeming with life,
But only the knife releases the tomb,
Liberating succulent flavours,
To see the world splitting - exposed.

Alexander Carden (10)
Beaudesert Park School

GUESS MY NAME?

I am not a native of chilly England,
But mostly come from warmer New Zealand.
When divided, I bleed trickling green blood,
I am as large as a toddler's firmly clenched fist.
My outer layer is unshaven,
With an emerald-brown hide.
My insides taste sharp and squidgy,
To a fly I may seem like a giant, hairy earth mound.
I am like a prison cell,
With my miniscule black pips locked up inside.
I am a kiwi.

Lydia Rogers (9)
Beaudesert Park School

GIRL IN A GARDEN - TWO VIEWS

Seen from above,
The red, silky strands are waving as
The arms swing jauntily.

Seen from above,
The house slopes slowly and smoothly down,
To keep the liquid from staying on.

Seen from above,
The green orb hangs,
As it ripples in the breeze.

But when you get down,
The hair is raw and hard,
As the arms swing awkwardly.

But when you get down,
The roof is not smooth, it is all ill-mannered,
The water crashes off, not smoothly this time.

But when you get down,
The tree is spiked and has sunk to the floor,
There is no waving of branches, it is still.

Edmund Arbuthnott (10)
Beaudesert Park School

PASSION FRUIT

Ball of sweetness,
A mini world,
Wide beaches of green seeds,
Whirling seas of yellow juice.

Mouth-watering, succulent,
A fly's feast,
Rough . . . no soft,
A healthy treat.

Nettle Grellier (9)
Beaudesert Park School

WHEN UP IN A TREE

When up in a tree,
The lion is harmless,
It's only a small cat.

When up in a tree,
The wolf is an innocent dog,
Just waiting for a stroke.

When up in a tree,
A zebra is purely a horse,
That you know and ride.

When down on the ground,
The lion is brutal and dangerous,
It pounces and kills.

When down on the ground,
The wolf is ferocious,
It hunts you for food.

When down on the ground,
The zebra is scared of you,
So it kicks and bucks.

William Boyes (10)
Beaudesert Park School

SEEN FROM IN SPACE

Seen from in space,
The world is a swirl of green and blue,
Like a tiny marble in a sea of black.

Seen from in space,
The sun is a swirling, whirling ball of gas,
Exploding as if it were an everlasting bomb.

Seen from in space,
Mercury is a tiny blue sphere,
A pearl in a never-ending blackened space.

Seen from in space,
I am an insignificant dot,
Barely visible in a universe of nothingness.

George Lloyd-Jones (10)
Beaudesert Park School

POMEGRANATE

Golden russet tones,
As colourful as autumn,
You wear a pointed wizard's hat,
But are as round as a ball,
Raindrop seeds glitter like jewels,
Edible football,
Fruity leather,
Cloying as sugar,
Pomegranate puzzler.

Ned Falconer (9)
Beaudesert Park School

IN THE CITY!

From a plane,
A city is a mass of skyscrapers
As high as the clouds.
Smoke rising from factories,
Ferries travelling back and forth,
With little figures scurrying around.

But when you get down,
A city is smelly and murky,
Tramps begging for food,
Unkind people shouting,
Children screaming.

Seen from above, the city is beautiful,
But when you get down,
It is a mass of shops and cars.

Max Radford (10)
Beaudesert Park School

PINEAPPLE

The sweet smelling,
Prickly leaved,
Delicious tasting,
Leaf sprouting,
Hillside topped,
Beauty of Africa,
Grown like a sacred fruit,
A beautiful ovoid,
With fragrant character.

Roanna Castle (9)
Beaudesert Park School

POMEGRANATE

A small red sun,
Came down from a tree,
I was sitting near it,
When it fell beside me.

I picked it up
And there I found,
Some small red seeds,
All squidgy and round.

They looked like red rubies,
Moist and clear,
So I picked them up,
Nibbling without fear.

Its texture was soft,
I spat it out,
For I knew,
Without a doubt

That this strange fruit,
From high on a tree,
Was not a taste
That pleased me.

Gus Slator (9)
Beaudesert Park School

MY LION

Lions are big, small and wide,
Lions are fast, smooth and can hide,
But one is faster.

Lions have manes, scruffy and shabby,
Lions have manes, soft and scraggy,
But one is better.

Who is he? Which one is he?
Is he brown? Is he cream?
Is he clean? Is he mean?

With claws that are razor-sharp,
He is the
Lion of my heart!

Poppy Ralph (9)
Beaudesert Park School

WISHES

I wish for my family to never die,
So we would be very happy
And I'd never cry.

I wish I had lots of yummy sweets
And munch them up,
Like real treats.

I wish that I could help the poor
And knock on every single door
And give them lots and lots of help,
So they could live for evermore.

I wish my family and I
Could fly and whirl
And raid the sky,
Watching the aeroplanes go by.

I wish I had a kangaroo,
That would bounce all over the garden,
With me and you.

Olivia Maxwell (8)
Beaudesert Park School

WISHES

I wish my bed would fly,
I would visit the poor and bring them comfort,
I could go anywhere I wanted,
I would zoom through the clouds,
Everything would be tiny,
Warm wind would whoosh through my hair,
Sun dazzling on my face.
I wish my hamster would talk,
I would teach him what I learn in school,
I could talk to him when I am lonely.
I wish I had a magical potion,
To turn toys real, to talk and sing,
I would play games with them
And have teddies tea parties.
I wish I was a fairy,
With wings to fly through the countryside
And a wand to wave.

Clare Lamport (8)
Beaudesert Park School

A FLOWER

Seen from above a flower is slim and attractive,
Like a merry-go-round with a blossom of colour,
Whizzing round and round, again and again.

Seen from below it's quite a different sight,
Crammed with insects crawling all over it.
Until a bee comes along and lifts all the pollen out,
Then they fly away.

Julia Fish (10)
Beaudesert Park School

WISHES

I wish I could fly,
I would like to dance in the sky,
I could soar in the fluffy white clouds.
All the aeroplanes whizzing past me, noisy and loud,
I could see China, Australia and all the world.
All the trees were like curled-up old green peas,
The seas were the colours of green and blue,
All swirling, whirling with the twirling current,
I wish I could speak to animals.
The old sandy camels with all their humps and bumps,
To talk to them would be wonderful,
So I could hear all their camelly secrets.
I wish my family and friends would be happy
And live in peace for evermore.
No wars would come,
Everyone would be in happiness for ever and ever.

Gabriella Ford (9)
Beaudesert Park School

MY BEAUDESERT POEM

B   is for brilliant, the teachers and school,
E   is for education, the best - that's the rule.
A   is for athletics, good sportsmanship the key,
U   is for useful, that is what we must be.
D   is for duty - we must help mankind,
E   is for excellence, personal best we must find.
S   is for sincerity, we must all be true,
E   is for energy, no time to be blue!
R   is for religious, our success is all His,
T   is for the very best school that there is!

Julia Young (9)
Beaudesert Park School

PAPER AND PEN

Seen from above,
Plain white square,
Hoping to be used.

Seen from above,
In one cupboard,
On one shelf,
In one room.

Seen from above,
You can hear its crying calls,
Alone, flat, sad.

But from close up,
The white square
Is coming alive.

When you get closer,
A pen is near,
What colour? Blue, black or empty?

From close up,
The pen, the paper
Are a match,
Is the pen going to write?

Olivia Milligan (10)
Beaudesert Park School

MYSTERY FRUIT

The exotic look of your dry coat,
The swollen mini-mountains on your jacket,
The extended bristles of your stalk,
From an ant's eye you're an undiscovered tree.

Your musty contents,
A syrupy yellow mix,
Your moist, delicious fruit,
From an ant's eye a luscious bubbling mellow,
Full of fragrant fruity scents of you,
The pineapple.

Siobhan Harlow (10)
Beaudesert Park School

FROM ABOVE A RIVER

Seen from above
The river is a piece of wool winding round pin after pin
In and around, out and around

Seen from above
A stream's thread is thin, spindly
Crookedly slithering snake-like, in and out of obstacles

Seen from above
The swamp's mole holes sit muddy - lumpy
Murky water is bending in and out

But when you get down
A river's water gushes down bashing lonesome stones
Through a passage of trees

But when you get down
The stream is a muddy channel
No more impressive than a dirty ditch

But when you get down
The swamp is a pile of lumpy mud
Swirling slowly round and round.

Emma Burgess-Webb (10)
Beaudesert Park School

PINEAPPLE

Outside a cold, dreary object on a supermarket shelf.
Inside an adventure of sun and warmth waiting to be explored.
A bright and sunny island just waiting to be opened,
A reminder of the tropics, a thought out of the rain.
A taste that does not expire,
A hand that pulls you into the luxuries of the world.
Just sitting in a supermarket . . .
Just sitting . . . waiting . . . waiting . . .

Allegra Van Zuylen (9)
Beaudesert Park School

MAN OR FRUIT?

As the knife sinks into the pip-filled flesh,
You hear the high-pitched screaming
Of someone in pain.
But still the knife is slicing,
Death is coming closer,
The screaming stops
And on the plate lies a body,
Alive no more.

Miranda Elvidge (9)
Beaudesert Park School

FIRE

Out comes the cold ashes,
Like a cloud threatening to burst.

In goes the curvy kindling,
The warming wood to follow.

After that comes rigid fir cones,
Which brighten the night with light.

Flames rush out like fraying thread,
What a soothing sight.

Annabel Ricketts (11)
Beaudesert Park School

PAPAYA

The fresh green ball lay there,
It had a scratchy tickly feeling of a fat pear,
It began to fall open as the blade slipped down,
A sunrise of orange and crimson dawned,
Around the black pebbles in a fleshy lake,
It's soft to taste and so tempting to take!

Scorching hot weather was where it came,
With sandy hot beaches . . . here's not the same!

Rosie Gordon-Lennox (10)
Beaudesert Park School

KIWI

Succulent and juicy,
With a green furry-fox skin,
Seeds like the black night,
With no moon in sight.
Running with emerald blood,
Fragranced with fruit,
Under a dark skin,
Lies a watery paradise.

Helena Maxwell (10)
Beaudesert Park School

POETRY WRITING

Poetry writing can be fun,
when you're outside and under the sun.
The words don't always have to rhyme,
but if you want, they will sometimes.
Don't forget syllables and punctuation,
they can get you in a real frustration.
When you're annoyed and need a rest,
just take a break and leave the pest.
But when you're alone on a rainy day,
don't ring up your friend and ask to play.
Get out your poem and start to write
and before you know it, you'll have worked all night.
Soon you'll have finished when all is done,
that's the time you can have some fun.

Alex Warner (11)
Beaudesert Park School

THE SOUND OF WATER

You hear the plippity-plop of the rain,
Running down the windowpane.

The dripping sewers down dark and deep,
Where nobody would dare to peep.

Explosions of water out of the sea,
Where some people hate to be.

The poisoning tankers splash into the sea,
Where all the fishes swim with glee.

Look after your water from the smallest drip,
Don't use the oceans as a rubbish tip.

Emma Bevan (10)
Beaudesert Park School

WISH POEM

I wish I had a chainsaw,
I would cut down all the dead trees,
I would make my garden beautiful.

I wish I had a potion which made people live forever,
I would give it to my family,
I would give it to my friends.

I wish I was the best footballer in the world and the richest,
I would be on TV,
I would help the poor.

I wish the world would live in peace,
There would be no fighting,
There would be no terrorists or wars for evermore.

Oliver Gardner (9)
Beaudesert Park School

SEEN FROM ABOVE

I looked down at the rugby pitch,
With the winter sun behind me,
The flags on the posts flapping,
As the ball flies through the minute H.

Seen from a plane, the cricket field looks like
A round parcel with a green tag.
The pavilion like a huge splodge of Marmite.

Seen from above, the pitches are different,
But when you get down below,
It's all normal again.

Felix Sowerbutts (11)
Beaudesert Park School

THE OCEAN

Seen from above,
The waves gallop along,
Like a race of horses.

Seen from below,
The waves crash at you,
Like an angry giant stomping.

Seen from above,
The fins of sharks and whales' tails,
Submerge into deep water.

Seen from below,
The little fish play about
And swerve fast through the coral.

Seen from above,
The seals dive in
And bark to attention.

Seen from below,
The seagulls sweep towards you,
Then you see their little feet splashing about.

Milly Bruce (10)
Beaudesert Park School

SEEN FROM ABOVE

Seen from above
The city is a bunch of leaves.
The people are drops of heavy water.

Seen from above
The trees are bundles of ripped-up papers.
The particles of wood are roughly pulled with the current.

Seen from above
The factories are a drip of liquid.
The power plants are zapping solid.

Seen from above
The city is a chaotic area.
The people are gigantic rocks.

Seen from above
The trees are a colony of troops.
The bits of wood are half the size of me.

Seen from above
The factories are sculptures of the world.
The power plants are like the Twin Towers.

Alex McIntyre (10)
Beaudesert Park School

ABOVE

Seen from above,
The clouds are a white fluffy sheet of cotton floating on a bed,
That is never made.

Seen from above,
The Earth is like blobs of ink scattered along a ball of paper,
That is never cleared.

Seen from above,
The mountains are like broken glass on a crisp white floor,
That is never swept.

When you get down,
The clouds are a dusky plain, like the darkness of an attic,
Never entered.

When you get down,
Earth is a boy's play-set filled with chaos
Of never-ending war games.

When you get down,
The mountains are like bubbly sherbet on a tongue, but . . .
Never tasted.

Pandora Turbett (11)
Beaudesert Park School

WISHES

I wish I could fly,
I would jump out of the car and glide over the traffic jams,
I would be silent floating through the cool breeze.

I wish everyone was happy,
The people would always be smiling,
The people would always laugh.

I wish no one would live on the streets,
No one would starve,
No one would get ill.

I wish there were no such thing as diseases,
No one would die because of diseases,
No one would weep because people die.

Rachel Smith (9)
Beaudesert Park School

ON A ROOFTOP

Seen from above,
The fields are like a patchwork sheet,
Lying still and calm on a bed.

Seen from above,
People are like tiny ants,
Carrying their food to their home.

Seen from above,
The cars are like a multicoloured piece of paper,
Changing its shape continuously.

Seen from below,
The fields are like a jungle,
Desperately needing to be cut.

Seen from below,
The people are chatting and laughing loudly,
Like a bunch of hyenas ready to fight.

Seen from below,
The cars are hooting and polluting the air,
Like some people vandalising walls with graffiti.

Laura Burridge (11)
Beaudesert Park School

WISHES

I wish my dad's father came to life,
So my dad could see him again
And so I could know him.

I wish I had a house with secret rooms,
When my friends come they would think it is boring,
But then I would show them the special places,
The rooms would be like Harry Potter rooms
And would be all warm with a fire.

I wish I had a pencil case,
That did all my work,
It would have days off when I had to get the stuff out of it.

I wish I had James Bond's car,
So I could go to war without being seen,
I would get a medal all the time,
I could fire at people.

I wish there was no such thing as war,
The world could be in peace
And terrorists didn't knock down the Twin Towers,
I wish there was peace all over the world
And everyone could be friends for ever and ever.

Cosmo Warner (9)
Beaudesert Park School

WISHES

I wish my daddy's back would get better,
I would have much more fun playing with him
And if it did, I would be very happy.

I wish that I could fly,
I would really like to zoom over fields
Houses, parks and my school.

I wish my dogs could speak,
They could tell me jokes and we could play games
And jump on the trampoline.

I wish I had some magic dust
To tidy up my room,
Then it would sparkle and twinkle
And glow like the moon.

Poppy Stirland (8)
Beaudesert Park School

WISHES

I wish poachers would stop killing innocent animals
Stop killing elephants for ivory and rabbits for coats

I wish I could be an imaginative inventor
I would invent a brilliant buzzer
So children didn't have to put their hands up
I would invent a useful pen with a pencil and rubber

I wish I could talk to animals
I would learn all about them
I would keep it a big secret

I wish I had all the James Bond gadgets
On my phone it would have a laser
And a screen with a pad to control my car

I wish the world would live in peace
There would be no fighting
There would be enough food for poor people.

Max Brodermann (9)
Beaudesert Park School

WISHES

I wish my sisters, brother and I all had ponies to ride,
With tack and grooming kit and stables to sleep in,
On the field down the lane.
I would ride my pony down to Brimscombe Stores
To buy bread and milk.

I wish my family could stay alive forever,
So that they can see their great-great-great-great grandchildren.

I wish I had a money box that was always full,
So that I could give money to the people who need food,
Drink and a place to live,
I would spend some on my family and me!

I wish that whenever I step into a forest,
Jungle or a wood, all of the animals came to me,
So that I could play, stroke and talk to them.

Lily Haycraft Mee (8)
Beaudesert Park School

FAIRIES

Where do fairies go to
When stars come out at night?
They gather all together
And dance in the moonlight.

Their pretty wings flutter,
As they skip between the flowers.
Round and round the fairies go,
Singing for hours and hours.

Perhaps you've even heard them,
Just before you go to bed.
Perhaps you've even seen them,
Flying above your head.

But always, always remember,
That fairies are sometimes there
And if you ever see one,
Please try not to stare.

Emma Clark (9)
Beaudesert Park School

TAKE HIS BODY BUT LEAVE HIS SOUL

Take Grandpa's body away but leave the soul,
let him smoke his pipe and sit in his old chair,
he's always in the air around me.

He will have his normal cup of tea, sugar, milk and cream,
he's always got his own theme,
so make me feel his love still in me,
take him but leave his soul.

We tried to fight the illness away but it did stay,
it lurked about, not caring the amount of people it scared,
it crept around on the ground, like a hungry wolf in the night.

But for Grandpa, there is a light through the darkness,
Heaven's beam,
so goodbye Grandpa,
take his body but leave his soul.

Hermione Corfield (9)
Beaudesert Park School

MY FUTURE

What will be here in the future?
Will the water still be cool and deep?
Will the air still be cool and breezy?
Will horses still be able to gallop about the fields?

Or will the fields be covered in tar?
Will the fresh pure fruit still be there
Or will they cut them down
To make way for a smoking fume factory?

Will the dark blackbirds still be able to fly
In such a blue sky?
Will the lovely smell of flowers still exist
Or will the fumes make a foul smell everywhere?

Will the fresh water of lakes still be here
Or will the water no longer be pure?
Will there still be colourful fish
Swimming in the deep blue sea?

Will the boats and the harbours still be there?

I hope so,
Don't you?

Emily Maggs (9)
Beaudesert Park School

THE PIG

Rolling around like a pea,
Fat and chubby, filled with glee,
Chasing his tail round and round,
Wondering what he has found.

Hairy body, pink and plump,
Tangled up in a lump,
Running around in the sty,
Trying to catch a tiny fly.

Sebastian Stafford (10)
Beaudesert Park School

THE MOURNFUL TRAMP

A tramp stared sadly at the sky
'Why, o why, o why, o why,'
He began to cry
He tramped along the busy street
Cold blue colour spread over his feet
Lots of people passed him by
Then he took a whiff
Luxurious smell of apple pie
His mouth started drooling
His eyes grew bigger
He hopped up and down like bouncy Tigger
His heart started thumping
Tabeet, tabeet
He waved his arms and stamped his feet
The wonderful smell of apple pie
Why, o why, o why, o why!
He tramped along the street once more
Back to the place he was before
His tummy rumbling of hunger and bore
Now the sun's down
The tramp asleep
His heart still thumping
Tabeet, tabeet.

Charlotte Brind (11)
Beaudesert Park School

DADDY IS A STAR

Oh Dad, you were so brave and strong,
When desperate cancer came along.
It was hard, it was bad,
For us it was really sad.
Dad had to always go to hospital, Mum had to go too.
I miss you, I will and I always do,
But now you're safe in the sky
And I know in my heart you'll never die.

Tilly St Aubyn (9)
Beaudesert Park School

THE ROSE

Its fiery-red petals glisten with raindrops
And as the rain comes pattering down,
It doesn't harm a leaf on the beautiful rose
And as I watch,
The rain leaves a wonderful glow
That will never fade
And will stay in my heart forever.

Elizabeth Morley (9)
Beaudesert Park School

THE POLAR BEAR

The padding of the paws,
To the rhythm of the beat,
The howl of the breath,
To the tapping of the feet,
The wagging of the tail,
Like an icy ball of snow,
Where is he going?
None of us dare to know.

Hunting through the Artic,
Blending in so white,
Not even seven hunters
Can reach their staggering height,
The sun is now arising,
Although it's still so cold,
The polar bear moves quietly,
Noble, fat and bold.

Anna Lloyd-Williams (11)
Beaudesert Park School

SCHOOL DINNERS

Smooth or sticky
Nice or icky
Lumpy custard, gone-off mustard
It gets worse every day
Even when I'm away
The smell is horrid
Like mouldy porridge.

Sophie Lousada (9)
Beaudesert Park School

THE PARROT

The parrot roams free and wild,
In the rainforest so damp and mild.

One parrot is reluctantly grounded,
Suddenly with nets she is surrounded,
But then with a roar and swipe
Of a claw, a tiger breaks her free.

Rhianna Evans (9)
Beaudesert Park School

The Storm

Spears of rain slash across your face like a cold, sharp knife
And whip and slap your eyes till they water

Blasts of wind play with your hair like an inquisitive child
And claw your face with giant bear's paws

Flurries of leaves snap at your heels like an unfriendly dog
And scuttle like rats back into the night

Clashes of thunder rumble like a volcano erupting
And crash, showing no mercy to the cowering world

Shafts of lightning split the sky in two
And shatter the gloomy darkness

The storm has moved on
The world is quiet now, so calm, so still

Peace.

Rachel Sykes (11)
Beaudesert Park School

Dibble And Dell

Two pairs of eyes, yellow and green,
Two noses, pink as can be,
Mouths mewing endlessly,
Soft fur winds between your legs,
Paws gently pummel your lap,
Tails twitching in the sun,
Purring deeply with contentment,
Are,
Dibble and Dell.

Harriet Dembrey (10)
Beaudesert Park School

THE CLASSROOM

The coat dangles longingly on a peg
The poster hangs as straight as a leg
Eek eek, the teacher's desk goes
As the swing door begins to close
The chairs lay scattered across the floor
But that all changes when he opens the door

A shadowy figure
Dressed in stern clothes
Opens the door
I stand on my toes
Now the finger begins to rise
(And the mouth opens very wide)
That is when the talking died
People cry
Detentions fly.

Thomas Dauncey (10)
Beaudesert Park School

THE FOX

He emerges at the fall of day,
Hunting down his feeble prey,
Amongst the woods he skulks around,
Burrowing deep beneath the ground,
He pounces on his weedy dupe
And gulps it down just like it's soup,
Prowling around the trees he goes,
How he survives, no one knows.

James Priest (10)
Beaudesert Park School

THE SPIDER

The spider lurks in the deep shadows,
He scuttles, silently, swiftly and stealthily
Towards the fine silky strands of his web.
When he has reached his destination,
At his glistening home,
He hangs, suspended in the air,
Waiting, just waiting, for an innocent victim,
To fly, very much invited, into his lair.
Time flies by, as does the creature,
Who is welcomed at his dwelling.
He wearily consumes his food with great difficulty.
As the sun falls and the eerie darkness replaces it,
So the spider's day ends.

Tom Morley (11)
Beaudesert Park School

MY BLACK CAT

My black cat
Sits on its mat
She goes to sleep
Dreaming deep
She loves some milk
Her fur's like silk
She wags her tail
And licks her fur
She likes chasing mice
And thinks it's rather nice
She pounces and jumps
And plays with her prey.

Issy Tanner (9)
Beaudesert Park School

A DARK NIGHT

Milky moon shimmering in the gloomy sky,
Why do you light up the night?
The leaves that laugh and sway with the wind,
What makes you so happy?
Impenetrable pond glittering in the moonlight,
Tell me how you sparkle?
Cunning creatures lurk in the shadows,
Why are you so sly?
Devastating quietness has taken over the night once again.

Katherine Lindemann (11)
Beaudesert Park School

WHAT HAVE YOU DONE?

I walked down one morning
On a cold winter's day
To find my little sister
Running away

With a smile on her face
She gave a large shout
I wondered what was wrong
So I chased to find out

I had her backed in a corner
She yelled for her mum
But before she came running
I saw what she'd done.

Freddie Gardner (10)
Beaudesert Park School

COLOURS

Brown is the tree that is so strong,
Blue is the sea, clear as air.
White is the sugar on a bun,
Orange is the great big sun.
Green is the grass we tread on so much,
Grey is the rain-cloud lurking in the heavens.
Red is for death, danger and blood,
Yellow's for happiness, joy and love.
Gold is every pirate's treasure,
Silver is the grand queen's pleasure
And black's the night sky.

Fred Miles (10)
Beaudesert Park School

TEACHERS

Teachers here, teachers there,
Teachers everywhere.
Bells ringing in my ear,
Some teachers fill you with fear.
Some kind, some grumpy,
Some are short and rather stumpy.
Others thin, others fat,
One hit me with a bat.
This is a school
Where teachers rule!

Alice Railton (10)
Beaudesert Park School

THE WIND

The dark night is still, but not for long,
The clouds fill the sky with pitch-black wool.
Leaves start to fly above our heads,
Animals and humans trying to keep warm.
Wind blowing, trees falling down,
Animals running for shelter.

Hours later birds are calling,
Sun appears very soon,
Children running out to play,
Tree trunks snapped,
Squirrels collecting nuts,
Calmness is finally here.

Emily Thomas (10)
Beaudesert Park School

MY MUM

My mum is cuddly, warm and nice,
Being happy and kind is her main device,
Willing to cook delicious food
And never, ever get in a horrible mood.

My mum is always helping and ready to share
And never growls like a bear,
Takes me on shopping trips
And never lets my eyes drip.

Georgia Mancroft (9)
Beaudesert Park School

SCHOOL CLASSROOMS

Boring teachers,
With ugly features,
Bullies pounding,
Instruments sounding,
Goody-goodies writing,
Big boys fighting,
Broken desks
And classroom pests.

Teachers screaming,
Good boys gleaming,
Silly boys are acting like fools,
This is what it's like at ordinary schools.

Finn Sowerbutts (10)
Beaudesert Park School

THE HUNTER

Deep in the jungle the lion roars,
He senses danger more and more,
The jungle is alive, the animals wake,
This danger is sighted and with it all
A shot tore past the lion's head,
With growling and roaring, the lion prowls,
Towards the intruder who fires his last shot,
A thud hits the floor,
Was it the man or the roar?

Sam Browne (10)
Beaudesert Park School

PASSION FRUIT

Glistening oyster-like,
With a red royal edge,
Pure pink close to the red
And glowing pearl white inside.

Wet and juicy then pink and red royal again,
Yellow as an afternoon's rays,
Hard and potato shaped on my outer side,
Growing on a shrub amidst the Caribbean.

Anna Lamport (10)
Beaudesert Park School

THE YOUNG BOY NAMED DAN

There was a boy called Dan,
He was a great big fan
Of Gloucester Rugby Club,
With players he really did love.
Every time they play,
There's always a big crowd
And every time they score,
They shout out really loud.
When the game is over,
We're heading to the bar,
They're singing Wild Green Rover
And Jesus Superstar.
Now it's time to go,
We don't live very far,
It's a good job I've got legs
Because I haven't got a car.

Sean Rudge (8)
Calton Junior School

MY DREAM MERMAID

The beautiful mermaid that lives in the sea,
Has golden hair and is different from me,
She has a swishing tail that flaps in the waves,
As she wanders through the rocky caves.

The mermaid's bed is glistening sand,
The sparkling grains are soft in her hand,
Her lovely voice has an echoing sound,
It reaches creatures all around.

The rippling waves that crash the rocks,
Often ruin her pretty locks,
The colourful fish like to play,
Talking to her makes their day.

The cold and salty sea is her home,
She's happy sometimes, but all alone,
I wonder if she exists or not?
I hope she does, because I like her a lot.

Satya Talwar Mouland (9)
Calton Junior School

RORY, THE TIGER

Mane is like a fiery ball
Mane is like a fiery ball
All the way round its neck
Roar is louder than a high-pitched whistle
Body is like a patched quilt
Pounces along when catching prey, tasty
Tail is as long as a giraffe's neck.

Joshua Jones (8)
Charlton Kings Junior School

LEMONADE

Lemonade is nice, though it can be fizzy,
Don't know about you, but it makes me dizzy.
A little girl called Mary found it out quite quickly,
Now she's a little pale and feeling a little sickly.
But one sunny day in midsummer's May,
She was a little ill on some golden hay.
Now for the rest of her life she never drinks
Fizzy lemonade, although that's what she thinks.
Next day she went to a party
And had a great big yellow Smartie.
Although it was nice to eat,
It was not such a pleasant treat.
Inside the Smartie, it was fizzy
And once again, she was dizzy.
This was the end of a girl called Mary,
All she drinks now is milk from the dairy.

Abbie Dawson (8)
Charlton Kings Junior School

MY CRAB

My crab
is snippy and
Scuttles   nippy and shuffles   Scuttles
across the sand like
an acrobat. Pincers like fingers
and its shell is like an
Scuttles   egg shell. Slippy, slimy like   Scuttles
a wet towel, wet tiles.
That is my crab. That
Scuttles   is my crab indeed!   Scuttles

Jack Howell (7)
Charlton Kings Junior School

4T CLASS POEM

I've met a young boy called William Palmer,
Now he thinks he has a lama.

Apparently there's a girl called Lucy Merry,
Once she was sick on a ferry.

I remember a girl called Mia Dodds,
Now she eats sea pods.

She goes to school every day,
But she is always missing her lunch play.

There's a boy called Joseph Scase,
He always asks me to do up his lace.

I know a boy called Matthew Diesel,
His favourite meal is roasted weasel.

I've seen a boy called Luke Drinkwater,
He is already married and has a daughter.

I've heard of a girl called Megan Reid,
She's in a race and in the lead.

My teacher is called Mr Theedom,
All he wishes for is some freedom.

Now my story is finished and done,
But don't worry, it is only the first one.

Abigail Sheridan (8)
Charlton Kings Junior School

4T CLASS POEM

I know a boy called Joseph Scase
Who managed to win a chicken race

I also know a girl called Lucy Merry
Who went abroad on a private ferry

Have you heard of Benjamin Haines
Who really likes the programme, Trains?

Remember the boy called Kyle Read?
He really liked the sunflower seed

You know a boy called William Palmer
I think he works as a pheasant farmer

I know a headmaster called Mr Moore
I just remembered, he broke the law

There is a boy called Christopher Brook
Who was really interested in the fishing hook

Have you heard of Shaun Overthrow
His little brother is a little low

I also know a boy called Luke Drinkwater
All the time he's got a daughter

I see one of my friends from 4T
I have to go, it's 10 past 3.

Jacob Stevens (8)
Charlton Kings Junior School

4T CLASS POEM

There is a boy called Overthrow,
He looks like he's going to overgrow
And also a girl called Eve Dimery,
Her skin is all clean and shimmery.
Then there is a boy called Christopher Brook,
Whenever I see him, he has a book.
A swell girl called Mia Dodds,
Who dances like fairy seed pods.
Also a teacher called Mr Theedom,
Who dreams, thinks and longs for freedom
And a friend called Holly Wright,
I think her mother works at night.
I know a boy called Matthew Diesel,
His favourite animal is a weasel.
Then there's this boy called Joseph Scase,
Who lost his teddy in a chicken race.
So there's most of the class and an extra bit,
I'm just an ordinary girl and nothing more of it!

Megan Reid (8)
Charlton Kings Junior School

4T CLASS POEM

I know a boy called Joseph Scase
Who was involved in a murder case
He has a friend called Alice Bray
And why does she always have to pray?

After this, there's Jacob Bailey
Who's always in the Daily
His best friend is William Palmer
Who wants a job as a chicken farmer

I know a man called Mr Theedom
And all he wants is his freedom
As you can see, that's all from me
In the wonderful class 4T.

William Palmer (8)
Charlton Kings Junior School

ANGRY BULL

Jon painted his car bright red
Because he was visiting farmer Jed
Jon realised he was being led
To a really tough bull's nesting shed
Farmer Jed came out and saw
His best friend all burnt and sore
Jed sent Jon into casualty
'Oh Jed,' said Jon, 'can they save me?'
'I'm afraid I do not know, my friend
But I can tell you're going round the bend.'
Soon Jon was out of pain
But now Jed's being really vain
'Hmm,' said thoughtful farmer Jed,
'Yes dear, I do want my bed.'
The next day Jon came back
He met a young man who he called Jack
They went for a ride in Jon's red car
And found themselves in a fish bar
They both went home in Jon's car that was red
On their way, they met farmer Jed
Then all three found they were being led
To an incredibly tough raging bull's shed

Never paint your car red
Because if a bull's nearby, you will end up dead.

Eve Dimery (8)
Charlton Kings Junior School

4T CLASS POEM

I know a boy called Joseph Scase
I caught him in a crime database

I know a girl called Lauren Shipley
I've seen her dog, it's called Nippy

I've met a boy called William Palmer
I heard he's a pig farmer

I've met a girl called Alice Bray
I heard her mum ran out of pay

I have a friend called Shaun Overthrow
I've met his brother - he keeps low

I have a friend called Holly Wright
And her father is a knight

I've got a teacher called Mr Theedom
And his best friend gave him freedom

I'm in a class called 4T
I'm going, it's ten-past three.

Luke Drinkwater (8)
Charlton Kings Junior School

CAUTIONARY TALE, OUCH!

I know a soldier called Joseph Scase
He was involved in a murder case
Found a grenade pin in his pocket
Blew his arm out its comfy socket
Arm went flying like a UFO
Landed on a big black crow

Unfortunately, it killed the bird
Then it got trampled by a buffalo herd
Joseph got called back to the war
He found it a great big bore
Then he got shot in the head
Everyone said he was truly dead.

Jacob Tait-Bailey (9)
Charlton Kings Junior School

4T CLASS POEM

I know a boy called William Palmer
I think he has a job as a pheasant farmer

Do you know this girl called Mia Dodds?
She likes climbing on very big logs

I also know a girl called Holly Wright
I think she likes the colour white

Have you seen Christopher Brook?
He is a really excellent cook

I've seen a boy called Shaun Overthrow
His little brother is a little low

Have you met someone called Matthew Diesel?
He really likes chasing weasels

My friend who is named Kyle Reid
I think he's in very bad need

These are my classmates of 4T
Now I am buzzing off like a bee.

Marko Andjelkovic (8)
Charlton Kings Junior School

4T CLASS POEM

I know a boy called Kyle Read
In his shed, he has a steed

I also know a boy called Luke Drinkwater
All the time, I think he has a daughter

There was a boy called Chris Brook
He was in a film called Captain Hook

There is a boy called Joseph Scase
He lost his arm in a murder case

I know a girl called Holly Wright
I know that her father is a knight

I remember a boy called William Palmer
I know he is a pheasant farmer

It's the end of this poem as you can see
Got to go because it's ten-past three.

Warren Cannon (8)
Charlton Kings Junior School

4T CLASS POEM

I know a girl called Mia Dodds,
She went to Holland to get her clogs.

I also know a boy called Luke Drinkwater,
I always think he has a daughter.

I remember a boy called Joseph Scase,
He lost his shoe in a race.

I'll always remember a girl named Grace,
She lost her pace in a cross-country race.

I know a girl called Holly Wright,
I always think she has a knight.

I remember a girl called Megan Reid,
Who always picks up green, green weeds.

I know a boy called Kyle Reid,
In his garden he plants some seeds.

These are my friends in 4T,
Made by me, Lucy Merry.

Lucy Merry (8)
Charlton Kings Junior School

4T CLASS POEM

I know a boy called Joseph Scase
I think he makes roller skates

I also know a headmaster called Mr Moore
I think he has broken many a law

Once a boy called Dinnen Griffiths
Destroyed a little town called Fiffiths!

Once a girl called Emma Gosling
Ended up doing a lot of grovelling

Once a boy called Jacob Tait-Bailey
Woke up at six o'clock daily

I know a boy called William Palmer
Who now wears solid bronze armour

I also know a boy called James Gassis
Who brought up a lot of gases.

Joseph Scase (9)
Charlton Kings Junior School

MY BEST FRIENDS

My best friend is:
Alice Bray,
Who loves playing with sloppy clay
And there's Abbie Dawson,
Who only reads about Cam Lawson.
Who likes Mia Dodds?
She loves kissing frogs.
Who plays with Megan Reid?
Who is not fussy and is easy to feed.

Who sits with Lucy Merry?
Who would like a nice strong sherry.

Who likes Christopher Brook?
Everyone says he's a great cook!

These people are my best friends
And I know my friendship will never *end!*

Lauren Shipley (8)
Charlton Kings Junior School

LEAF POEM

Smooth
Soft
Like a blackbird
Catapult to the ground
Swish down like a rocking horse
Scatter in the air
They are so smooth
They scatter around
Swish down
Smashing ring.

Jack Wickens (7)
Charlton Kings Junior School

LION

Mane like a horse,
Mane like a horse,
Growls like a dog,
Looks side to side quickly,
Eyes shine,
Licks like a cat,
Very fat,
Pounces like a cat,
Twitches when prey is near,
Rips meat like a cheetah,
Moves rapidly,
Sharp claws,
Like a tiger,
Cautious movements,
Action,
Moves swiftly,
Claws scratch,
Catches fast!

Mary Woolley (8)
Charlton Kings Junior School

FLAMINGO POEM

With a heart full of heat
Foggy eyes
Dips his black beak and shuffles
Eyes that gaze
Vast, handsome
Lifting his leg
Like a hockey stick.

Georgina Shill (7)
Charlton Kings Junior School

AUTUMN POEM

Moving
like
rain on
the
window

Woodland
pattern

Twirls
like
the wind

Flutter down
from
the
old tree

Crunches
like
Rice Krispies

Swishes in
the air
coming
down

Soft like
tissue

Leaves
making
autumn.

Kate Buckingham & Emma Lawrance (8)
Charlton Kings Junior School

LEAF

Like
Crunchy
Cornflakes
Smells
Like a lit
Candle
Crumpled
Tree trunk
Like a flamingo's
Feet

The
Stalk
Is like the
Wiry legs
It's golden like
Treasure. It
Smells like wet, smelly
Carpet
It looks like
Scarlet petals

When
You put
It on your ear
It is like a
Crunchy headphone
When you feel the leaf
It crackles.

Natalie Lewis (8)
Charlton Kings Junior School

4T CLASS POEM

I know a boy called Kyle Reid,
When he went gardening, he dug up a weed.

I know a boy called Christopher Brook,
Who likes to try and hook the crook.

I am a boy, Daniel Mubarak,
I like to eat lovely fresh carrot.

I also know a boy called Joseph Scase,
Who hides a grenade in his back base.

I know a boy called Ben Haines,
Who likes to lock himself up in chains.

I know a boy called William Palmer,
His dad isn't a snake charmer.

These are my friends from 4T,
Goodbye from Daniel, that's me!

Daniel Mubarak (8)
Charlton Kings Junior School

4T CLASS POEM

I know a boy called Luke Drinkwater,
All the time I think he has a daughter.

I also know a boy called William Palmer,
I know he wears golden armour.

Once there was a boy called Joseph Scase,
He lost his teddy in a case.

I know a girl called Alice Bray,
She went away at lunchtime today.

I also know a girl called Lucy Merry
And she ate a poisonous berry.

These are my friends from class 4T,
It's over and out from Amelia-T.

Amelia Tinton (9)
Charlton Kings Junior School

MY FRIENDS IN CLASS 4T

I know a girl called Mia Dodds
She went to Holland and brought me some clogs

I also know a girl called Holly Wright
Who always repeats her name at night

Have you seen the girl, Lucy Merry
Who has a best, best friend called Kerry?

I've heard of a boy called William Palmer
I think he has a job as a pheasant farmer

I know a girl called Alice Bray
Who could not tell the time of day

I also know a man called Mr Theedom
Who liked books but could not read them

These are my friends in 4T
And the person who wrote this is me!

Sasha Jacombs (8)
Charlton Kings Junior School

4T Class Poem

I know a boy called James Gassis
He was a pain for the lasses
He had a friend called Ben Haines
He had a dog that was called Lanes
I also know a girl called Holly Wright
She likes to repeat her name when dreaming at night
I think I have a friend called Joseph Scase
When he walks, he takes a long pace
I know a girl called Lucy Merry
She's got a boyfriend, his name is Perry
Our class teacher, Mr Theedom
Likes to have lots of freedom
Here is me, Gabrielle Burge
When I see frogs, they make me urge
These are my friends from 4T
Goodbye for now from Gaby B.

Gabrielle Burge (9)
Charlton Kings Junior School

Fear

Fear jumped into my veins,
Ordering me to feel pain,
He shook me,
He hit me,
But never did he speak,
He pulled out my happiness,
Making me shiver and tremble,
I was in a world of despair,
For I had let him win.

Adam Wood (10)
Coalway Junior School

THE BEACH

I ran across the sandy shore,
Then paddled in the sea,
I sat there bathing on my towel,
While the sun shone down on me!

A sandcastle then I built,
A sandcastle tall and strong,
But then, behold, the tide came in,
So it didn't last too long!

Then the sun said goodnight
And the moon came out to shine,
So I went home, I went away,
But that memory . . . is mine!

Bethanie Burford (11)
Coalway Junior School

THE CAT

A loud miaower
A mouse catcher
A waste eater
A tail swisher
A basket stepper
A bird scarer
A bed disturber
An amazing pouncer
A lap napper
A cream guzzler
A tree climber
A quick runner
A brilliant fighter.

Jake Marlowe (10)
Coalway Junior School

HISTORY OF THE GNOMES

Once long ago
In a faraway place,
There lived little gnomes,
A remarkable race.

They were led by a man,
King Terry was his name,
They lived in perfect harmony,
Until the sorcerer came.

The only thing the gnomes feared
Was an ugly witch,
Her name was angry Agnus,
A pretty awful snitch.

They liked to wind up Agnus,
Until she said, 'That's it!
I'm fed up of the pesky pixies,
I'll blast them all to bits!'

So one cold winter's day,
She set out on her broom,
Flying in the sky,
She caused trouble and doom.

She turned the happy gnomes to stone,
Starting with King Terry,
One froze playing, one froze drinking
And one stopped eating berries.

So when you throw your football
Into the garden gnome,
Think about the little people
Who lost their little homes.

Edmund Rayner (10)
Coalway Junior School

MY WITCH BREW

She lived in a house with her little black cat
She wore a coat and a black, pointed hat
Her name was Jemima, her cat was called Bubble
But all her spell casting resulted in trouble
Her broomstick had crashed, her nose had grown straight
When invited to covens she always came late
She sometimes attempted to cook evil brew
But it always went wrong and tasted like stew
At last she decided that things had to change
So she brought a new broomstick, top of the range.

Amy Pearson (11)
Coalway Junior School

A DOG

A big biter
A bone chomper
A high jumper
A good hider
A tail wagger
A deep sleeper
A biscuit eater
A quiet sleeper
A kennel liver
A hat chewer
A newspaper fetcher
A sloppy eater
A loud barker
A cat chaser.

Hannah Worgan (10)
Coalway Junior School

WINTER'S HERE AGAIN

Her branches lent in the dark
Gripping soft white snow
Winter's here again

He shone down on the crying tree
Trying to comfort her
Winter's here again

Hand in hand the mountains stood
There, hugging each other
Feeling the snow as it bashed down on them
Winter's here again

The poor fence stood there in the snow
Calling out for help, but nobody, nobody comes
Winter's here again

Laying down there, the pond is
Sleeping, waiting for winter to go by
Winter's here again.

Sophie Giles (10)
Coalway Junior School

EASTER

E   aster's come once again,
A   ll are getting fat,
S   ummer's on its way.
T   eacher's getting Easter bunnies,
E   ggs are getting eaten,
R   eady to be demolished!

Jade Davis (11)
Coalway Junior School

THE CAT

A mouse catcher,
A bin scratcher,
A tail swisher,
A tuna fisher,
A bird killer,
A water spiller.

Layla Dovey (11)
Coalway Junior School

LIMERICK

For homework, class seven got this,
'Write me a limerick,' said Miss.
So I worked for ages,
On lots of blank pages
And finally said, 'Here it is!'

Lindsey Fowler (11)
Coalway Junior School

A DOG

A hard biter,
A tail wagger,
A fast runner,
A high jumper,
A good hider,
A loud barker,
A bone chomper,
A biscuit eater,
A kennel liver.

Laura Knight (10)
Coalway Junior School

JUST JACK

Everyone thinks that I'm just Jack
The boy with ginger hair
But I must tell you something
It's a secret I must share

At night when you are all asleep
I climb out of my bed
I take off my pyjamas
And put a costume on instead

I open up my window
And look up at the sky
I hold my breath and count to three
And then I start to fly

I am a superhero
I fly all through the night
I try to rid the world of crime
I sometimes have to fight

When at last my work is done
And I can do no more
I fly back home to bed
And put my costume in the drawer

In the morning Mum wakes up
And she turns on the light
Just a few more minutes Mum
I saved the world last night

I haven't got a superhero's name
And really I don't care
'Cause everyone knows that I'm just Jack
The boy with ginger hair.

Jack Bullingham (8)
Foxmoor School

MY GRANDMA

When my grandma drove her very first car,
She crashed it into a bus,
The driver phoned for the police to fix it,
They kicked up such a fuss!

When my grandma stoked on her first train,
She started to cry when it started to rain,
The driver tried to calm her but all in vain,
The train fell, never to rise again.

When my grandma flew her very first plane,
The radar system was such a pain,
She just couldn't see,
Why it made a noise like a bee
And why sparks flew left and right!

When my grandma sailed her very first boat,
She climbed the mast and fell off again,
She couldn't swim
And wouldn't float,
She drowned due to her thick fur coat.

Whatever you may say about my grandma,
True, she never could drive a car,
But saying else is going too far;
'Save the history',
The papers said
And it is true
What they all say –
Of her history, there is no clue.

Samuel Thompson (10)
Foxmoor School

THE FOOTBALL RAP

I'm a footballer
I play for a team
I play right-wing
And I'm really keen

Do ya wanna play
And have some fun?
Score some goals
And then we run

We score some goals
Sometimes one
Sometimes a lot
And sometimes none

Do ya wanna play
And have some fun?
Score some goals
And then we run

We go training
On Wednesday night
Play a match
Like dynamite

Do ya wanna play
And have some fun?
Score some goals
And then we run.

Nathan Buckland (10)
Foxmoor School

SCHOOL!

School!

I think school
Is such a bore!
No time for shopping,
Just loads of hopping.

I hate school!

I wish we didn't have ICT,
Disco dancing would be better for me.

I hate school!

Mathematics is such a bore,
Why can't we do so much more?
Like a fashion show or something new,
Oh, I don't know what to do?

I hate school!

We have English,
Which makes me tinglish,
Why can't we have a pool?
That would be so cool!

I hate school.

Candice Francis (9)
Foxmoor School

MY GREAT GRAN

My great gran is really great,
She's 87 years old,
Her face is brown and crinkly
And she always feels the cold.

My great gran's got lovely teeth,
Although they're not her own,
She keeps them on the mantelpiece,
Between the clock and phone.

She has to draw her eyebrows on,
With a pencil that is grey,
Her sight is not that good these days,
She did them *green* one day!

My great gran knows lots of things,
Because she is so old
And when I'm at my great gran's house,
I'm always good as gold!

Joanna Bullingham (9)
Foxmoor School

A LADY OF FRANCE

There was an old lady of France,
Who taught little ducklings to dance,
When she said, 'Tick-a-tack!'
They only said *quack*,
Which grieved that old lady of France.

Sadie McDermott (11)
Foxmoor School

LIVING MY LIFE

When it rains, I feel sad
But when it shines, I feel so glad

I play football up in the field
I score lots of goals and hold up the shield

I ride my bike through the park
But Mummy says, 'Not in the dark.'

I ride my scooter to the shops up the street
It's fish and chips night and that's our treat

I go to bed and watch the bright stars gleaming
In a few minutes, hopefully, I will be dreaming.

Kyle Yam (9)
Foxmoor School

THE TIGER

The tiger, lord of the jungle,
Stalks in his camouflage and blends into the long, golden grass,
His eyes like eclipses in the sky,
His beautiful exterior brushes the bark of the trees,
He pushes through the wild bushes
Until he gets to a water hole where he laps the cool water,
A gazelle draws near to quench its thirst,
The tiger hides perfectly merged till his victim draws near,
He pounces on his prey and has his feast,
He leaves the rest to the scavengers,
The huge pack of hyenas and vultures,
The regal tiger rests, this powerful hunter.

Jessica Line (10)
Foxmoor School

MY NEW BABY

I'm so excited,
I just can't wait,
Soon it'll be here,
Not long now,
Late in Feb,
Yes that's right,
I wonder what it'll be,
A boy or girl?
I'll have to wait and see,
Three days later,
It's here,
It's here,
It's a boy,
Hooray,
Hooray,
Now we can play.

Sophie Martin (11)
Foxmoor School

SCARY THINGS AT NIGHT

You go out at night
The problem is, there is no light
Ghosts and grizzly bears
Vampires, mummies
And things with no hair
Things that go, *raaa*
Things that go, *boo*
But the scariest thing . . .
Is you!

Jasmine Ebbrell (11)
Foxmoor School

JAM DOUGHNUTS

There it sits
That small, drowned in sugar, dough lump,
Looking at me innocently
In my hands it sits, *all mine!*
It's full of temptation screaming for me to eat it
I can't take anymore of this waiting
I sink my teeth in, oh delicious, scrumptious and sweet
It makes me dissolve on the spot
Another bite
I've reached it! *The jam*
I look at it, that bleeding heart of sweet, red liquid
Freeing the jam from its dough prison
I dive my tongue into the pool of scarlet syrup
It is just so much fun!
I want to savour it, but I can't
The last mouthful, and then
All gone!

Benjamin Curwen (10)
Hatherop Castle School

WHAT IS IT?

This animal has big, sharp claws so you had better watch out,
He might get you,
He lives in the forest and he hibernates for six months in the winter,
He could kill you if he wanted,
If you poke him, he will kill you,
So you'll have to run as fast as you can,
Can you guess what this animal is?

That's right, it is a bear.

Carys Chalklin (9)
Hatherop Castle School

A WINTER POEM

Wonderful winter, shining in the frost,
No care in the world, just free to let it snow,
Penguins and polar bears ice skating, while the humans
Are resting and trying to keep warm, robins are hopping and
Bobbing around with tiny footmarks in the snow and
Huskies running, sharp holly edges turn to ice while the
Dew is setting on the sparkly grass, humans tucking up,
In bed ready for the next cold day, morning now is
Here, the rain is beating hard, the snowdrops are all now
Melting into nothing but water.
The humans awake, the moonlight still shines,
The children come in with their gloves and hats,
Oh, they're sent away with their heads drooped low.
The snow has turned to pure slush, the ice is still,
Freezing by the minute. The mistletoe is turning
Dry, the humans are sitting by the fire having a hot
Drink and a biscuit. The wellies are full of water.
The sky is grey and the day is gloomy.

Harriet Bishop (11)
Hatherop Castle School

THE ELEPHANT

The elephant is a unique beast,
That wanders on the Earth in feast.
A quiet, lumbering, genuine creature,
With many a hair, many a feature.
The wonderfully grey beautiful skin,
Always fat, never thin
And while human beings run on,
The elephant lumbers, big and strong.

Tom Dyer (9)
Hatherop Castle School

WINTER SNOWMEN

W hite, fluffy snowflakes falling from the sky,
I cicles hanging like stalactites on the tree above,
N umb, nippy noses turning red,
T urn around, so excited to see snowflakes falling down,
E normous snowflakes falling from the sky,
R osy cheeks are shivering.

S nowballs are wonderful to make snowmen,
N ippy snowflakes, pile them together,
O h! We're nearly finished, I just need the head!
W inter snowmen have to have a nose,
M erry snowman sitting on my lawn,
E xciting little snowman with a very jolly face,
N aughty children throwing snowballs!

Rosie Williams (9)
Hatherop Castle School

ARE DRAGONS AND WITCHES REAL?

Are dragons and witches real?
I think they have small meals,
Witches have very funny heels.
The dragon rings with his wings,
Instead of his fingers.
I think he lingers
Around every single day.
The witch looks at her ring,
To see what to bring
To the tea party.
I think dragons and witches aren't very hearty.

Georgia Hind (8)
Hatherop Castle School

ANIMALS

Monkey swinging through the trees
Rhinos in the outback
Crocodiles in the water
Whales in the ocean
Birds in the air

Elephants in the long grass
Lions lurk in the sun
Polar bears in the cold snow
Camels in the sandy desert
Fish float downstream

Flamingos paddle in the water
Ostriches run wild
Zebras in the long grass
Owls hoot in the trees
Wolves growl and bare their teeth.

Sophia Mackay (8)
Hatherop Castle School

FOOTBALL

F   ootball, football is great
O   ver the crossbar, nearly in
O   ver the top, the ball spinning
T   ipping in the top, seeing over heads
B   ursting through the players, zoom
A   ll the way through, going fast
L   osing control, passing through open legs
L   inesmen running, saying offside.

Stuart Jones (8)
Hatherop Castle School

KITES

A kite is always darting and swooping around in the air,
Floating, diving as well,
If someone does not want to come, just drag him or her
To a hill and a big open space where you can fly a kite.
Flying a kite makes you happy, perky and chirpy,
Kites are sometimes dazzling down at you.
Kites make you cheerful,
Kites are mostly whizzing around.

Philip Purry (8)
Hatherop Castle School

SINGING POEM

S   is for scales,
I   is for imaginative,
N   is for noises that singing always makes!
G   is for great choirs,
I   is for improvement,
N   is for notes that make your throat go sore!
G   is for gigantic that a choir can really be!

Elizabeth Reavley (8)
Hatherop Castle School

WORLD

W   onders throughout the world,
O   n one lovely hot air balloon,
R   unning out of time, got to get to work,
L   ullabies all the way,
D   ucking under clouds in the angels' world.

Adam Gerges (8)
Hatherop Castle School

HORSES

White horse,
Black horse,
Carry me away,
Over the hills and far away.

White horse,
Black horse,
Over the rainbow,
Here we go.

Big horse,
Small horse,
Pretty you can be,
Take me home with you.

White horse,
Black horse,
White mane and tail,
Black eyes dazzle the sky.

White horse,
Black horse,
Carry me away,
Over the beach and far away.

White horse,
Black horse,
Over the black sky,
With us.

Big horse,
Small horse,
Coloured you can be,
Over the moon with me.

White horse,
Black horse,
Brown body and hooves,
Grey legs like me.

Felicity White (9)
Hatherop Castle School

HUNTERS IN THE SNOW

The brave, cold hunters,
Travelling in the bitter breeze,
They hear the whistling of the birds,
They give commands to their dogs,
They get the wind blown in their faces,
Brave,
Fierce,
Strong.

Samuel Evans (8)
Hatherop Castle School

DOUGHNUT HEAVEN

There before me a plump, sugary doughnut.
So tempting to sink my teeth into.
The fresh doughnut smell fills me with joy.
As I take my first bite the jam squidges out
And the sugar covers my lips.
The round, chubby lump of jam-filled dough has gone
So quickly.
Now I only have the thought of the doughnut left.

Fleur Adderley (10)
Hatherop Castle School

MY TEDDY

My teddy is soft,
My teddy is cuddly,
At night he stares,
Through big, green eyes.

His fur is a light gold colour
And he smells of lavender,
I like to take him
Everywhere I go!

On spooky nights like Hallowe'en,
When ghosts creep all around,
I hug him tight, his silky fur
And whisper, 'I love you!'

Dawn Stevenson (9)
Hatherop Castle School

PENS

Red pens, yellow pens
Big pens, small pens
Writing pens, gold pens
Gel pens, fountain pens

We use pens every day
We use them for work and use them for play
Felt-tip pens we use to colour
Biro, teachers use them every day

Pens, everybody uses a pen
From baby to adult
We use a pen,
Pens!

Timothy Knight (9)
Hatherop Castle School

THE TIGER

The tiger,
a stripy, red-eyed beast,
walking through the jungle,
looking for a feast.

The zebra,
grazing by some grass,
not knowing that a tiger
is likely now to pass.

The kill,
the tiger runs at speed,
grabs the stripy horse
and starts to happily feed.

The tiger,
walks home to his mate,
licking round his lips,
not telling of his fate.

Georgina Atherton (11)
Hatherop Castle School

SEASONS

S   is for seasons which rule our world.
E   is for Easter which is in spring.
A   is for autumn.
S   is for Saturn which has no seasons at all.
O   is for oranges which are used for Christingle which is at Christmas.
N   is for nuts which are gathered in autumn.
S   is for spring when all the flowers start to grow.

Harry Chalklin (9)
Hatherop Castle School

FOOTBALL

Football is a game of strategy and skill,
The record football score is 36-nil.
Playing in the mud or the green short grass,
Delivering that super fifty yard pass.

Curling from a free kick, swerving round the wall,
Flying through the air, into the net it falls.
The crowd goes wild, the players scream,
It is all like a magical dream.

The final whistle blows, the players celebrate,
Everyone is happy, they all become good mates.
The crowd goes home, with smiles on their faces,
The players hug the manager and everyone embraces.

Edward Smith (11)
Hatherop Castle School

THE WILD HORSE

The wild horse as fast, as fast as light
Storming through the wood
The trees are rustling
The lake is shimmering
The wild horse just ignores this

The wild horse stops in front of the lake
To have a drink of water
Nobody looks after the wild horse
Except himself
But everybody loves him.

Rosie Poole (9)
Hatherop Castle School

COBY, THE DOG

Coby, the dog, soft and cuddly,
Coby, the dog, smooth and warm,
Brave and handsome too,
I love Coby, the dog.

Coby, the dog, browny-gold,
Coby, the dog, with a hard black nose,
Silky fur too,
I love Coby, the dog.

Coby, the dog, with a big red collar,
Coby, the dog, lives with me
He's my Coby, the dog.

I love Coby, the dog.

Claudia Holt (9)
Hatherop Castle School

HUNTERS IN THE SNOW

Hunters like silhouettes battling the icy-cold snow,
Strong, fierce and mysterious.
Gunshots all around,
Fierce howls from the wolves,
The barking of the dogs,
The birds calling to each other,
The hunters shouting with the breezy weather in their faces.
The hunters could hear the sliding of the skates,
The crackling fire,
Crunching in the snow.

Tom Perkins (8)
Hatherop Castle School

THE MYSTERIOUS RIDER

I saw a mysterious rider
With a horse as black as night
As he rode along the pathway
His green cape waving in the wind
The rider's black stallion
As wild as wild can be
Running along the pathway
Like no one was riding him
The rider looks like his horse
Black and mysterious
Is it real
Or an illusion?

Maddie Forman (8)
Hatherop Castle School

SMUDGE, THE PUPPY

Smudge, the puppy, cute and adorable
Smudge, the puppy, furry and soft
Cuddly and sweet as she sleeps

Smudge, the puppy, warm and smooth
Brown and white in the snow
Soft nose and brown eyes

Smudge, the puppy has silky fur
Runs fast, runs slow
That's my one and only puppy.

Arabella Pollock (8)
Hatherop Castle School

RASPBERRIES

R   aspberries are as sweet as sugar
A   raspberry can grow wild
S   unny days make them ripe
P   ink as a piglet
B   abies blow raspberries
E   arly in the summer
R   ed means really ripe
R   ipe as a red apple
I   ce-cold raspberry juice
E   at them all you want
S   uddenly they go away to come back another day!

Amy Worsfold (9)
Hatherop Castle School

SILENT HUNTER

As darkness falls
Over the fields,
A silent hunter
Swooping, looping,
Down, down,
Down to the mouse
And then it ascends
Gracefully up to its
Feeding post for the
Rest of the night,
Eating his catch.

Lauren Barnes (10)
Hatherop Castle School

MY PUDGY LITTLE DOUGHNUT

It's sitting there all round and fat
With dark holes full of jam
Layers and layers of white fluffy bread
I just can't resist the taste

My teeth are sinking to the middle
They're touching everything
I've got it! I've got it!
The jammy taste in my mouth

My hands are tingling
I've lightened up
The joy is all around me
I need to get another bite
I just can't pull back.

Clementine D'Arcy Clark (10)
Hatherop Castle School

DOUGHNUT

Chubby and plump,
Layered in sugar just like glittering snow,
I have got to eat it, I can't wait any longer,
I stick my tongue into the delicious, oozing, blood-like jam,
It has almost gone, the last bite of the yummy dough,
Laden in that frosty sugar
And has gone,
It gives you a very happy feeling,
When you eat a doughnut just like that one.

Emily Chambers (10)
Hatherop Castle School

A VIEW ON LIFE

Life is like yeast,
A fat, greedy thing,
Growing, consuming
And meeting its end.

The path of life
Is never easy,
For yeast consumes
Its fellow man.

The value of life,
Belongs to the owner,
The value of death,
Belongs to the gone.

Bryony Logan (11)
Hatherop Castle School

MY LITTLE FRIEND

One day I see a little man
With sticky, jammy eyes
His fat, round body is covered in snow-like sugar
He's just so tempting
I have to sink my teeth in
One bite and the jam bursts out
Mm, it's delicious
I have one bite left
It's all gone, but look – I found another one!

Catherine Walpole (10)
Hatherop Castle School

THE LIGHTS IN THE SKY

The man looked up
There were lights in the sky
Ten there were
All shining white

The people looked down
Then, strangely, they found
Thousands of them
Men on the ground

Humankind looked up
Puzzled, he was
The reason for this
Was simply because

The aliens looked down
From their lights in the sky
Irrelevant, they thought
And now they must fly.

Alexander Davis (9)
Hatherop Castle School

GO-KARTING

Hear those roaring engines whizzing past your ear
And the screeching tyres making a loud cheer,
Skidding round the corner, gives you such delight,
Turning on your flashlights, they're so very bright.

With daring splendour the atmosphere's filled,
Don't go too fast though or you might be killed!
Race your very fastest on the final lap,
Then you will be the only winning chap!

Elliot Greenwood (11)
Hatherop Castle School

DARKNESS

I'm walking through a dark wood,
I hear a noise . . . who could be there?
Just silence like a grave.

I keep walking down the dark woodland path,
I hear a screech far away . . . what can it be?
I pause for a while,
Silence meets my ears.

I carry on,
Then a rustling nearer than before
And a cat appears . . .
Have you ever wondered what's in the darkness
Around you?

Bryony Smith (9)
Ingleside PNEU School

FLOWERS

Tulips underneath the bowers,
Daffodils the merry flowers.
Roses growing straight and tall,
Pansies the most colourful of all.
Bluebells deep inside the woods,
Foxgloves with their delicate hoods.
Geraniums in their bunches all,
Lilies brighten up your hall.
Flowers, gardens, pretty sights,
Always such a great delight.

Emily Blampied (9)
Ingleside PNEU School

YESTERDAY'S PARTY

Old sweet wrappers and forgotten crisps litter the floor,
A 'Happy Birthday' sign hangs by the door,
A pile of presents lie on a chair,
Before there were children,
Now nobody's there.
The bouncy castle's up,
That's a good thing,
But even that's lost its fun,
Like a bird with one wing.
The magician is smoking in the drive,
But there is one thing I'll remember,
From this moment on,
Today I am five.

Maddy Turner (10)
Ingleside PNEU School

ALL ALONE

You're walking along, all alone
And then you hear a mutter and a groan,
You look around to see if anyone's there,
But there's no one anywhere.
Though you keep on walking,
But your step is slow
And the fright inside you seems to grow
'Cause you know someone's following you.
It's just you don't know who . . .
You don't know who!

Yasmin Lester-Powell (10)
Ingleside PNEU School

LIFE

Every day is joy
Like playing with your favourite toy
Keeping healthy every second
That most of us have reckoned
What a lovely world it can be
But not as easy as squishing a pea.

Sophie Jones (10)
Ingleside PNEU School

THE MAD SCHOOL

The sticky, muddy grass has clung to the ground,
Tyres swinging side to side on a very blustery day.
Glass windows smash against the wild wind,
Trees crash against the rusty fence,
Children laugh playing their secret game.

Liam Bale (9)
Leighterton Primary School

HAPPY CHILDREN

Children play on the climbing frame
They run like rockets
Children get into fights
A lovely breeze blows across the playground
Teachers moan at children
Crying children bursting out.

Aaron Ryan (8)
Leighterton Primary School

A WINTER PLAYGROUND

The wobbly bridge rocks side to side in the breeze
The children are smiling happily
Swaying lonely on their bare branches shine on winter days
Children happily skip across the playground
The swings swinging above the ground
All the grass dances in the soft winter breeze
Children run quickly across the playground
Crying children cry loudly as the blood drips from their cut
Damp wet benches are dripping in the rain
The wet trees swirling in the wind
Boys and girls hopping along the chessboard.

Olivia Carter (8)
Leighterton Primary School

THE PLAYGROUND

Balls jumping wet and beautiful,
Feet dancing carefully,
Playing in the wendy house,
Children jumping happily,
Big feet hopping,
Dry grey playground
Trees swaying when children are playing
See-saw creaks slowly
Teacher shouting
Wet climbing frame
Trees swaying
Teacher racing boys and girls.

Emily Clout (8)
Leighterton Primary School

PLAYGROUND

Long benches, wet all over
Tall climbing frames, rusty and red
Sun shining brightly
Swing on the slippery monkey bars
See-saw creaking slowly
Children shouting happily
Play in the little wendy house
Feet colourful, fun to follow
Obstacle course hard to complete
Grass wet, too muddy to play on
Fat ropes to swing on all around
Trees to climb on all about us
But best of all, the playground is a happy place!

Alexandra Reed (8)
Leighterton Primary School

THE STUNNING PLAYGROUND

The rusty swings creak loudly,
The dirty play house stands lonely,
Children scream horribly as the teachers look at their legs,
Everyone swings happily on the monkey bars,
People run around the playground laughing
Red balls jump up and down like the ground is too hot
The big see-saw grinds high and low
Teachers sit in the staff room drinking hot coffee
But at the end of the day the school is quiet.

Helen Jones (8)
Leighterton Primary School

THE MADNESS OF THE PLAYGROUND!

The old climbing frame sways,
Children swing bar to bar,
People swing on the rusty old tyres,
The grass sways in the order of the wind,
Children hop joyfully over the chessboard,
Large red roundabouts spin speedily,
Big wet benches lay bare and lonely,
Creaking see-saws rocking steadily,
Girls and boys laughing on blue bouncing space hoppers,
People struggling on slippery ropes,
Hopscotch fades quickly and wet,
Parents sitting waiting while drinking warm cocoa,
At the end of the day the playground waits longingly
For the next day to come.

Hannah Williams (9)
Leighterton Primary School

HAPPY AND SAD PLAYGROUND

People shouting 'Help' from the monkey bars,
Pushing happy chess pieces across the chessboard,
Little kids catch big kids,
Playing noisy football,
Crying loudly on the wet bench,
Swinging sadly on the rusty tyres,
Screaming painfully at the bleeding knee.

Guy Crick (8)
Leighterton Primary School

PLAYGROUND

Children laughing happily as they rush across the grass
The swings sway freely, hastily in the wind
On the grassy field, children run joyfully
The wailing wind rushes the world
Young children rush madly around the playground
Rusty, groaning swings hastily blow in the wind
The strong climbing frame holds as a child climbs
The wet cold bench creaks sadly
A child swings alone, sadly crying
Teachers sip tea silently, discussing events of the day
Children are hopping happily as the sun shines bright
All the children agree that the playground is obviously the best!

Laurence Webb (9)
Leighterton Primary School

A HAPPY PLAY TIME

The rusty swings lazily sway
All of a sudden there's an outburst of noise
As the children madly run out of their classrooms
The roof tiles shimmer in the faint sun
The breeze scatters leaves everywhere
Dodging the husky children
The bench creaks in its lonely corner
The bell rings and all the children silently line up.

George Rumney-Kenny (8)
Leighterton Primary School

SUMMER PLAYGROUND

Boys and girls rush to get the best space hopper,
Creaking seesaws rocking steadily
Happily jumping on colourful trampolines
Sweetly skipping round in big circles
Grown-ups sighing long sighs, pleading their children to come
Large roundabout spinning speedily
Trees swaying side to side in the rough wind
Teachers sit together with warm coffee in their hands
Dusty tyres swinging slowly
People holding tightly to the monkey bars
But best of all, the sun is shining brightly and sharply.

Beatrix Joyce (9)
Leighterton Primary School

CHAOS IN THE PLAYGROUND

Children are chasing bouncy footballs noisily
Falling over and screaming from bleeding knees
Some people are sliding unbalanced across the soggy grass
And getting muddy
One boy is on the wet bench and crying, lonely
Two people are swinging on the tyres sadly
Space-hoppers are blowing longingly in the wind
And this just shows the disasters of the playground.

William Bradley (8)
Leighterton Primary School

THE SUN

The sun from the east
Is a pale sun
A sun of kind gentleness
A sun of sleepiness
The sun from the west
Is a hurtful sun
A sun of fierce emotion

The sun from the south
Is a kind sun
A sun of laughter
A sun of wacky enjoyment

The sun from the north
Is a wild sun
A sun of pain
A sun of great strength.

Laura Radley (10)
Longdon St Mary's CE Primary School

JELLY

The jelly from the party
Is a wobbly jelly
A jelly of laughter
A jelly of fun and giggles

The jelly from the fridge
Is a shaky jelly
A jelly of sweetness
A jelly of kind taste.

Elizabeth Warner (10)
Longdon St Mary's CE Primary School

THE CAR

The car from the garage
Is a proud car
A car of speed
A car of power

The car from the dump
Is a crumpled car
A car of slowness
A car of badness

The car from the racetrack
Is a good-looking car
A car of smoothness
A car of technology

The car from the factory
Is a new car
A car of brightness
A car of elegance.

Tom Crutchley (11)
Longdon St Mary's CE Primary School

THE WEATHER

The wind from the north
Is a strong wind
A wind of strength
A wind of muscles

The rain from the east
Is a beautiful rain
A rain of friendship
A rain of love

The sun from the south
Is a friendly sun
A sun of joy
A sun of hope

The cloud from the west
Is a bold cloud
A cloud of courage
A cloud of bravery.

Sophie Larner (10)
Longdon St Mary's CE Primary School

THE TRACTOR

The tractor from the dump
Is a smelly tractor
A tractor of faith
A tractor of dashed hopes

The tractor from the factory
Is a cruel tractor
A tractor of power
A tractor with no heart

The tractor from the farm
Is a kind tractor
A tractor of friendship
A tractor of kind comfort

The tractor from the show
Is a posh tractor
A tractor of meanness
A tractor of brutalness.

Josh Scrivens (10)
Longdon St Mary's CE Primary School

THE FOOTBALL

The football from the match
Is a bouncy ball
A ball of energy
A ball of great power

The football after the match
Is a flat ball
A ball of injury
A ball of sadness

The football from the garden
Is a punctured ball
A ball of patches
A ball ripped by the dog.

Gareth Roberts (10)
Longdon St Mary's CE Primary School

CARS

The F1 from New York
Is a beastly car
A car of noisiness
A car of terrifying loudness

The estate car from Sweden
Is a lean car
A car of pride
A car of kindness

The coupé from Germany
Is a special car
A car of quietness
A car of friendly light.

Joseph Yeates (10)
Longdon St Mary's CE Primary School

SHIPS

The ship from the dock
Is a cargo ship
A ship of money
A ship of purpose

The ship from the port
Is a passenger ship
A ship of friendliness
A ship of kindness

The ship from the navy
Is a fierce ship
A ship of fury
A ship of decisiveness

The ship from the harbour
Is a fisherman's ship
A ship of silence
A ship of character.

Edward Cooke (10)
Longdon St Mary's CE Primary School

SILLY BILLY

There was a boy called Billy
His mum said he was silly
He stood on his head
And fell out of bed
Then he said, 'Mum, I'm illy.'

Jack Martin (10)
Longdon St Mary's CE Primary School

THE CLOUD

The cloud from the north
Is a black cloud
A cloud of darkness
A cloud of anger and death.

The cloud from the east
Is a gentle cloud
A cloud of peace
A cloud of smiling and joy

The cloud from the west
Is a fiery cloud
A cloud of hunger
A cloud of thirst and poverty

The cloud from the south
Is a soft cloud
A cloud of laughter
A cloud of hope and thoughtfulness.

Eleanor Kirby (9)
Longdon St Mary's CE Primary School

WATER

The water from the sea
Is a calm water
A water of laughter
A water of waves stroking

The water from the river
Is a rough water
A water of coldness
A water of forcing strength

The water from the pool
Is a warm water
A water of kindness
A water of friendship

The water from the Atlantic
Is a cruel water
A water of anger
A water of cold deepness.

Cherise Price (9)
Longdon St Mary's CE Primary School

THE SUN

The sun from the south
Is a fiery sun
A sun of hotness
A sun that burns you

The sun from the west
Is a soft sun
A sun of gentleness
A sun of warm kindness

The sun from the east
Is a shy sun
A sun of coolness
A sun of small smiles

The sun from the north
Is a nasty sun
A sun of cruelness
A sun of intense brightness.

Grace Woodward (9)
Longdon St Mary's CE Primary School

BIKES

The bike from the west
Is a good bike
A bike of skills
A bike of great haste

The bike from the north
Is a bad bike
A bike of slowness
A bike of laziness

The bike from the east
Is a diabolical bike
A bike of mischief
A bike of untidiness

The bike from the south
Is an excellent bike
A bike of wealth
A bike of huge brilliance.

Jude Wagstaff (9)
Longdon St Mary's CE Primary School

I AM PLAYING

I am playing, I am playing,
I am joking with my friends,
I am laughing out loud,
I am joyful without end.

I am saying, I am saying,
I am praying with my friends,
I am hoping this weekend,
That I can play with them.

Jasmine Quiney (9)
Longdon St Mary's CE Primary School

I AM DANCING

I am dancing, I am dancing
I am swirling on the stage
The lights are up above me
And the audience gaze
I am prancing over theatres
And twisting over seas
I am frolicking through the forests
And leaping over trees

I am dancing, I am dancing
On the thick sparkling ice
I am whizzing and I'm gliding
I think I'll do it twice
I am whirling and I'm twirling
In a jubilant display
I am as happy as a fairy
On a sunny winter day.

Rosanna Sinclair (9)
Longdon St Mary's CE Primary School

MY COOL GRANDAD!

Grandad is a fluorescent green
As soft as a furry sofa
Grandad's a strong shout
He's the steps to a sunshine pearl beach in Heaven
Grandad's as soft as a woolly jumper
He's the hot chocolate on a winter's day
Grandad's a furry koala
He's as hot as the boiling sun
And the best grandad in the whole
Universe!

James Purvis (10)
Lydney CE Primary School

THE WRITER OF THIS POEM
(Based on 'The Writer Of This Poem' by Roger McGough)

The writer of this poem
Is cooler than a bee
As funny as the joker
As pretty as can be

As quiet as a mouse
As bright as the sun
Is taller than a house
As fast as a gun

As thin as a stick
As outstanding as the teacher
As clever as a lick
As polite as a preacher

The writer of this poem
Is as funky as can be
'Cause the writer of this poem
Is beautiful *me!*

Amy Biddle (10)
Lydney CE Primary School

GRANDMA

Grandma is a light shade of blue
She is a comfy chair
Grandma is the hum from a hummingbird
She is a tree in the still wood
Grandma is a snugly woolly jumper
She is a cup of tea cooling on the table
Grandma is a summery butterfly
She is the wind swooping through the trees.

Christie-Anne Wayman (10)
Lydney CE Primary School

THE WRITER OF THIS POEM

(Based on 'The Writer Of This Poem' by Roger McGough)

The writer of this poem
Is smaller than a flea
As playful as the kitten
As funny as can be

As clever as a calculator
As busy as a bee
As dazzling as a star
As weak as herbal tea

As pretty as a princess
As bouncy as a spring
As messy as a pigsty
As sparkly as a ring

The writer of this poem
Is just as super as can be
You really have to meet her
That poet is Gabi!

Gabi Olley (10)
Lydney CE Primary School

MY BEST MUM

Mum is glittery gold
She is a soft pillow
Mum is a quiet mumble
She is a path in a winter wonderland
Mum is a warm winter scarf
She is a glass of hot chocolate by the fire
Mum is a scurrying mouse
She is a setting sun in the summer.

Stephanie Wilcox (10)
Lydney CE Primary School

WARNING

When I am an old woman, I shall wear hot pants
With a top that's too small and does not suit me
And I shall spend my pension on bags, clothes and champagne
And high-heeled shoes that are lush and say, 'No money for cat food!'
I shall go to the nightclub every night and go pole dancing
And do graffiti on my neighbour's wall!
Save all my money and go nightclubbing again
And wear rainbow colours to funerals.
I shall work in a hospital and say people have got broken legs
When they haven't.
But now I'm just a schoolgirl
Perhaps I should start wearing hot pants
So people get used to me when I am *old!*

Amelia Challenger (10)
Lydney CE Primary School

CHRISTMAS!

Christmas is here
Let's have fun
And play in the snow
With everyone

Make a snowman
While Christmas is here
And see everybody
Clap and cheer

Christmas is here
Let's play in the snow
With the Teletubbies and Po.

Ashleigh Bailey (10)
Lydney CE Primary School

REFUGEE

G oing now forever, never coming back.
O n to a different country, but what shall I take?
O bjects are nothing compared to love, like
eD ucation is more than food.
B angles can trade themselves to earn our money.
Y ou think, think, think, I won't be accepted in the world of safety.
rE jected in my own homeland, I have to go.

F orward I walk as a refugee.
O yo is the place to go, will I ever be
R eunited with my friends and family?
E ternity that will last forever.
eV entually I'll get home,
E vents that I will always remember.
R efugee, refugee for my life.

Nikita Salmon (11)
Northleach CE Primary School

ARTHUR THE SAD

Arthur is sad for
His lost sword.
He would be very bored,
Arthur walks to the lake,
He sees the Excalibur.
On a hand,
This sword is magical,
Arthur goes home with no scratches at all.

Jonathan Drinkwater (11)
Northleach CE Primary School

I LOVE YOU
(Refugee poem)

I will miss my family, but when I heard I was leaving
   I was devastated, disgusted, angry and furious.

L iving somewhere else was going to be hard, Mum was crying, she
   was scared, she was also frightened that she'd never see me again.
O pposite my house lived a girl, I knew she had just found out
   because I could hear people crying, her mum was devastated.
eV erything was different now, it seemed gloomy and sad. It seemed
   like someone had died.
E ven the children weren't playing, soldiers were marching around
   looking sad because their families may not survive.

Y ou would think the children were excited but they weren't, they
   were furious, they didn't want to leave, they wanted to stay.
O f course, when we got there, we were bullied but you couldn't
   go home and tell your mum because she wouldn't be there.
I U nderstand my mum's feelings because I felt the same.

Holly Gardner (11)
Northleach CE Primary School

WHAT I LIKE ABOUT MY KITTEN

The wet, pink, shiny glint on the nose of it,
The soft, ginger fur on it,
The bright lamp-like eyes on it,
The low, rumbling purr of it,
The high-pitched miaow of it,
The rough, warm lick of it.

Tom Hancock (10)
Northleach CE Primary School

REFUGEE POEM

I run for my life, as I hear the gunshots of death,
As I hear people going, dropping to the floor every second.
I run or I will be late for freedom,
I'm near freedom or pain.

Will I be happy or will I be miserable?
Can it be Hell? Could it be Heaven?
I'm looking for happiness.

I'm in this place called freedom,
It seems like a prison, but it's better than my home.
My beliefs are not welcomed, but the hatred and exclusion,
. . . is better than death.

Matthew Eames (10)
Northleach CE Primary School

BLUE SNOW

Why isn't snow blue?
Why isn't rain red?
Why are grasshoppers green?
Is it so they can't be seen?

Why do leaves fall off trees?
Why do birds have wings?
Why do clouds look like faces
And lots of other things?

Oliver Krisson (11)
Northleach CE Primary School

WHAT IS A POPPY?

What is a poppy? Some would say,
'A poppy is a sunset at the end of the day,
Over the poppy fields far, far away,
Where many soldiers, motionless, lay
And beneath the treetops the shadows play.'

What is a poppy? Some would tell,
'A poppy is a sign we all know well,
To remember the soldiers in Heaven no Hell,
Who went to the war with their lives to sell,
There on the poppy fields many fell.'

What is a poppy? I would have said,
'Purely a way to remember the dead,
With so many soldiers the earth was fed,
The poppy, bearing its petals of red,
The colour of life, blood . . . and death.'

James Ager (10)
Northleach CE Primary School

AN AXE HEAD

Some say just an axe head, but really much more,
Cast in a mountain, years before,
First as a buckle, then as a spade,
Then left as nothing, no real form,
Until more dwarves came and opened a door,
A door to working, a door to power,
A door to moving, hour upon hour.

But now I am an axe head,
But my thoughts tell me no!
I was cast in a mountain a long time ago.

George Dale (10)
Northleach CE Primary School

THE DEEDS THAT I HAVE DONE
(Based on 'Macbeth' by William Shakespeare)

Out blood out I say.
It is on my hands.
Although I get no wounds.
I did not touch thy weapon.
Why me, why me?
For I have not touched anyone.
My father is dead.
I am weakening.
My brain and body are weakening.
My soul is weakening,
But my guilt stays with me as strong as ever.
I'm afraid.
My guilt makes my brain ill.
My nightmares come and they never go.
Stabs come into my stomach
For I should be dead not them.

Lorna Rainey (10)
Northleach CE Primary School

LADY MACBETH SOLILOQUY

I cannot hide my guilt for what I have done.
Why am I guilty for what I have not done?
How can I see this blood when I have not done the deed?
Go away I cannot stand this anymore
Why does the torment me so?
My guilt is breaking out
Help me
Help my body
Help my soul.

Holly Phipps (11)
Northleach CE Primary School

THE SECRETS OF A WINDOW SHUTTER

I come from a tiny seed
Grown into a tree
Then cut
It smelt like flower blossom
It looked so happy and a fun place to be
Exploring, becoming famous
Also finding rare artefacts
My family are trees and mirrors are my brothers
The seeds were my parents
My enemies are the people who tore my family apart
I believe in predictions
Superstition and that one day I will be human
My hobbies are listening to secrets
And watching what evil deeds people do
I speak woodish, plank and treeish
I think I'll end
Being burnt in a crackling fire
Broken
Or worse sliced like soft white bread.

Michael-Sean Hurst (11)
Northleach CE Primary School

WHAT I LIKE ABOUT FOOTBALL

The bone-crunching tackles of it,
The fireball shots of it,
The top corner saves of it,
The shiny boots of it,
The halfway line shots of it,
You may score a goal at the end of it.

Steve Larner (11)
Northleach CE Primary School

THE GLEAMING ARMOUR

I come from fire and
I smell of a sweaty breeze.
Then every day I dream of
Becoming the world's most valuable thing.
My friend is a warrior and
My family is a big army of soldiers,
My enemies are spears and guns which
Come flying at me every second during wars or fights.
I believe in trying to save a man's life when they are
In danger of being killed and
All my hobbies that I have are fighting in wars.
My language is a high tingling voice.
My favourite food is blood.
Then sometime soon my
Life will come
To an
End!

Ben Miles (11)
Northleach CE Primary School

NOWHERE TO RUN, NOWHERE TO HIDE
(Based on 'Macbeth' by William Shakespeare)

Thy blood is following me,
My heart is losing its bounce
It will not leave my side
My guilt is written on my hands with blood
My crown is slowly tumbling
Into the hands of pure evil
My power is fading
My eyes are blurred
Blood is everywhere.

Rebecca Mills (11)
Northleach CE Primary School

LIFE

The sun, he smiles down on us,
Beaming with pride as he warms up the world.
The sun keeps us warm and alive,
If we had no sun, we would have no life!

Trees, they wave at us in the wind,
With pride at giving us oxygen and life.
Trees keep us alive.
If we had no trees, we would have no life!

The rain falls down and tickles us,
Giggling with pride
As it re-hydrates the world.
The rain keeps us hydrated and alive,
If we had no rain, we would have no life!

Jessica Phillips (11)
Northleach CE Primary School

LADY MACBETH

I repeat, get off blood, get off.
Why does thy blood never vanish?
I did not kill thee,
Instead I made it happen.
For I am faint and powerless.
My dreams are filling with guilt more and more,
For I am the evil one.
My eyes are weakening bit by bit.

Joseph See (11)
Northleach CE Primary School

REMEMBRANCE DAY

Remembrance Day, years of remembrance
The victories, the losses,
Red bloodstained poppies, being crushed
By falling bodies,
Crying families weeping for their loved ones,
The warming sound of silence.
The wars are over.
Families still waiting for familiar faces to return,
The red poppies rising, growing around dead bodies.
The muddy fields turning into a field of red,
We remember this time in 1945.

Jack Stevens (11)
Northleach CE Primary School

REFUGEE

I would hate to live in a different home
Changing schools, I would be alone.
My favourite toy I would bring,
Is a little round teddy that always sings.
I didn't want to leave my mummy,
She always said I was her honey.
When I went to school next day,
I shouted over to some kids, 'Can I play?'
Mum please come and get me, it's so scary,
They tell me to go on long walks which make me weary.

Latoya Evans (10)
Northleach CE Primary School

REMEMBRANCE DAY

The life of the people
Who died at war
Have risen again.
As their spirits walk
Before them.
As the spirits lead them
To their new life.

The spirits of the people
Who died at war,
Look down and see
The hearts of those
Who care for others
And take it to their souls.

The colour of blood
Is a dark red,
Like the petals of poppies,
As those who died
Lay crushing all the poppies.

Kelly Welch (10)
Northleach CE Primary School

ARSENAL POEM

Stunning Pires shoots like a star
While Henry shoots from far
Kanu's tricks are really cool
Makes any defender look like a fool
Bergkamp shoots from any direction
Doesn't even need a good deflection
All these strikes have a theme
They play for Arsenal, fantastic team!

Harry Wilkins (11)
Northleach CE Primary School

REFUGEE POEM

I'm out on the street,
I'm all alone,
I'm without a nearby phone.
I want to phone my family,
To see if they're OK,
Why is it me that has to pay?

I don't have any food,
I eat scraps off the pavement,
I don't have any transport,
I'm in an imprisonment.
I have to beg for money,
I only have a pound,
This is making me dizzy,
Going round and round.

Connor Harries (11)
Northleach CE Primary School

REMEMBER

Remember the death and the loss,
The sacrifice and the pain,
Sadness runs through people who have lost their love,
We sleep in peace thanks to people who fought.
New life sprang from the ground,
As the first flower came to life.
To show we remember we wear poppies
And put crosses in the ground,
To say we remember.

Melanie Norman (10)
Northleach CE Primary School

LADY MACBETH

Thou art my blood I can see
Get away thy blood go, go, go
You're making me feel ill
I see my spirit in my head
Why do I see blood when I did not
Kill these people?

There once was a king called Duncan
My husband had a friend called Banquo
The Thane of Fife had a wife and children
Where are they all now?

I see my hands shaking, I am weak
I see blood everywhere, I am scared.

Lauren Larner (10)
Northleach CE Primary School

LADY MACBETH

Thy blood taking over my life,
Guilt flooding onto the floor of my soul,
Go, go, go, however many times I wash they do not go,
I hate being queen. I hate being queen,
I did not commit a murder so why do I suffer?
Why doesn't Macbeth suffer?
Banquo's ghost still haunts me,
My brain is ill, the time is close to the end,
My soul is ready.

Eliot Binns (11)
Northleach CE Primary School

REFUGEE

R eady to leave my perfect life for somebody else's.
E verybody else has disappeared into thin air, I'm all on my own,
  nobody else to turn to.
F or everything I want to take is not possible.
U nited never with my family.
G one forever, not sure if I'll return.
E ven if I try to, I cannot change their mind.
E ncouraging myself that this isn't the *end.*

Virginia Chilton (10)
Northleach CE Primary School

COLD HAIKU

Children slide on ice,
Tumbling fast like young skittles,
Wrapped up in warm scarves.

Lizzie Hunt (10)
Oak Hill Primary School

THE CHRISTMAS TREE

Christmas lights glowing,
Pine needles sit like small spears,
Scent soothes your senses.

Duncan Hainsworth (10)
Oak Hill Primary School

ZEBRA KENNING

Horse liker
Lots of striper
Black and whiter
Non fighter
Stampede lover
Pony's brother
Nifty trotter
(Not a dotter)
Grass eater
Hoof beater
Lion fearer
Death nearer!

Enla Fees (10)
Oak Hill Primary School

AN OSTRICH KENNING

Long-necker
Hard-pecker

Tall-stander
Loves-lander

Orange-legger
Grey-featherer

Big-layer
Long-stayer.

Ben Johnson (10)
Oak Hill Primary School

A WOOLLY MAMMOTH

Hairy dresser
Big impresser

Standing tall
Above all

Tusken raider
Grass invader

Icy roamer
Big loner.

Thomas Howell (10)
Oak Hill Primary School

SATURDAY MORNING

Excitement
As children awake
Snow falls as morning dawns
Children watch the snow drop . . .
Then stop.
Wow!

Emily-Jane Harris (11)
Oak Hill Primary School

JANUARY HAIKU

Freezing flakes fall down.
Snow is like icing sugar,
Soft as a duvet.

Hayley Robinson (11)
Oak Hill Primary School

A KENNING ABOUT SNAKES

Clever hider
Non strider

Path guider
Strong glider

Desert dweller
Bad news teller.

Freddie Cooper (10)
Oak Hill Primary School

CHRISTMAS CINQUAIN

Surprise!
Grins on faces
Wondering what's in the
Long, bumpy stockings on the beds.
Come on!

Abigail Row (11)
Oak Hill Primary School

CHRISTMAS MORNING CINQUAIN

Mysteries
Await under
Bright-coloured tree waiting
For you and me – excitement grows
Quickly.

Robin Edgermorgan (11)
Oak Hill Primary School

CHRISTMAS CINQUAIN

Sparkling
jets of bright lights
beam through busy branches
below presents glow with surprise
then go!

Stephanie Mumford (10)
Oak Hill Primary School

IF I COULD FLY

If I could fly, I'd fly all day
Over the hills and far away
To many places, Africa, India and Australia too,
Where I'd see lions, tigers and possibly a kangaroo.

If I could fly to the top of the old church spire,
I would want to go much higher,
Over the smoking chimney tops I'd soar,
Until I'd go and explore far more.

If I could fly, I'd fly for fun,
Up to space to see the sun,
Then on past planets like Pluto and Mars
And find the way out to see the stars.

If I could fly to the end of the day,
I'd have to fly home if I remember the way,
By then I'd be tired, but I'd fly like the best,
So off to bed for a well-earned rest.

Thomas Walsh (9)
Querns Westonbirt School

SCARED OF THE DARK

I was in my room
When I heard a noise
It was coming from under my bed
The light was off and the door was shut
Thoughts of monsters and aliens filled my head
Under the duvet cover I slid
And silently covered my face
The hairs on the back of my neck stuck up
And my heart began to race
Across my room it tiptoed softly
Preparing to attack
It landed with a thud upon my bed
Panic over, it's just my cat!

William Lawrence-Mills (9)
Querns Westonbirt School

THE DARK

Along the dark corridor I tiptoe,
The corners are dangerous places,
I peer around to make sure it's safe,
Don't want to see any scary faces.
I'm scared because I fear a monster is near,
Just waiting to gobble me up.
I look left and right, how I hate the night,
I freeze and give a nervous hiccup.
There's nothing there, I run to my room
And into my bed I dive,
Under my blankets I safely snuggle . . .
. . . Phew! I'm lucky to be alive!

Joshua Wall (9)
Querns Westonbirt School

THE VISION NEXT DOOR

Hair, black as ebony,
Skin as white as snow.
Cherry lips as red as blood,
Cheeks, pink like a summer rose.

Eyes like stars in a midnight sky,
That twinkle when she smiles.
Tapered fingers, nimble, thin,
Silvery tears and a silent cry.

She hovers as she floats through the air,
In a flash, her presence is near.
You look at her,
But in a glimpse,
The vision disappears.

Stephanie Cowan (10)
Querns Westonbirt School

SILENTLY CREEPING

I'm silently creeping
While Mummy is sleeping
To look at the stars
Or maybe see Mars
The moon is bright
Black is the night
A dustbin clangs
Or vampire with *fangs!*
I scramble back to bed
And cuddle my brother Ed.

Ellen Franklin (9)
Querns Westonbirt School

SOUNDS OF SILENCE

Can you hear the leaves flutter, falling to the ground
Or the water as it freezes with the cold?
Can you hear the frost sprinkled lightly on the flowers
Or the red holly berries shrivel when they're old?
These are the sounds of silence.

Can you hear the fluffy clouds drift by
Or the stars twinkling on a moonless night?
Can you hear the butterfly sucking nectar from purple buddleia
Or the joy of a blind man when he regains his sight?
These are the sounds of silence.

Can you hear the light-footed pond skater across a rippleless pond
Or the frozen snowman as he melts in the warm sun?
Can you hear the summer season fading
Or the arrival of buds on the trees as spring's begun?
These are the sounds of silence.

Victoria Hilton (10)
Querns Westonbirt School

BUFFALO IN THREAT

I pound through the grass
And I whiz past
I cross a river
I run to save my liver

They eat
My meat
They wear my skin
If only they knew what fear I'm in.

Lena Reding (8)
Querns Westonbirt School

SOUNDS OF SILENCE

Can you hear the bitter frost creeping stealthily over the ground
Or the scarlet berries shrivel up when old?
Can you hear the buzzards soaring above the clouds
Or the unspoken fears of a knight so bold?
Can you hear the magic of a child's Christmas
Or the passing of time in a convict's cell?
Can you hear a mother's pain as she holds her starving baby
Or the fear of a bullied child that is unable to quell?
Can you hear the steady heartbeat of a hibernating squirrel
Or the tense determination of an athlete waiting for the gun?
Can you hear the Eastern sun as it warms the plains of Africa
Or the exhilaration of a competitor when the final race is won?

Florence Prosser (10)
Querns Westonbirt School

INDIAN HUNTER

Indian creeping
Buffalo sleeping
Spear aiming
Indian gaining

Silently he'll creep
On pitter-patter feet
Sneaking through the grass
He lets the minutes pass

When he thinks it's time
He fires!
Buffalo dead
Indians fed.

Isobel Holley (8)
Querns Westonbirt School

The Hunter

I'm hunting high and low
To catch a buffalo
I hear running hooves
Time for some quick moves

Stabbing animals with my spear
Especially lots and lots of deer
We will all have a feast
Of all the beast
I have caught this night

I've killed the buffalo
After hunting high and low
I did it!
Gosh the thrill
Of the kill
Is so very, very powerful.

Lucy Ibbotson (8)
Querns Westonbirt School

Treasure Map

Treasure map, treasure map,
Where are you?
On faded parchment paper,
With words of uncertain truth.

Which way are we to travel?
Which turns are we to take?
Be careful, pirates might track you,
If you're caught, you're sure to quake.

Georgina Cowan (10)
Querns Westonbirt School

THE WINTER MORNING

I wake up to see the misty, black winter's day and stay in bed.
I get out of bed to find the coldness of the winter air.
I get dressed and try not to have the freezing air to tickle my nose
                                    and to sense the cold outside.
I go downstairs and run outside not noticing at first how cold it
                          is outside and soon feel the coldness of the air
I look down on my already blistering nose and hands
Twinkling, shimmering diamonds
Scattered all around the frosted, cold, hard ground
The leaves are cold and hard
Now and then you feel cold
Freezing breath that looks like smoke rising to the already
                                    misty, big, black sky
Coming down and trying to flatten me
Suddenly it's freezing me to death
So I feel myself running back into the house
And running straight ahead to the warm welcome of the glowing fire.

George Mullen (8)
Rangeworthy CE Primary School

WINTER MORNING

Crunching leaves as you walk
Sky of colours, like a kingdom above
Icy trees full of beauty
Slippery diamonds of frost and sun
Puddles frozen like rivers of ice
Plants covered with frost like another world
Early in the morning a quilt of black.

Sophie Romain (7)
Rangeworthy CE Primary School

WINTER MORNING

Winter morning
I see, I feel the snow
I hear the cold breeze
And when all the trees
Oh, start to freeze
The mist of mists goes by
Oh why, oh why
The winter goes on by
Let us wait for next year now
And let the birds
Touch the sky.

Ruby Williams (7)
Rangeworthy CE Primary School

WINTER MORNING

Icy icicles on a frosty morning,
Clear blue sky,
You can hear
The birds calling
Shimmering diamonds
Smooth puddles
Glistening winter ice
It's a cold morning
Freezy, breezy morning.

Evie Guest (8)
Rangeworthy CE Primary School

A Winter Morning

A winter morning, trees are bare,
A cold nose, a cold cheek,
Trees covered in a coat of frost,
Trees look cold and miserable,
Little spikes of frost upon the gate,
A frozen pond, a frozen lake,
A cold, dark world in a case of whiteness,
The morning's cold and dark
And silent, just the odd cry from a freezing crow,
Puddles frozen and wet,
You can smell the cold, misty air,
The feel of the cold,
Taste the cold air.

Hannah Cornford (8)
Rangeworthy CE Primary School

Winter Mornings

Shimmering diamonds
Glistening on the ground
Bare trees rustling
Birds singing, frost clinging
Crunching leaves
The cold winter breeze
The colours in the sky are bluey, pinky, creamy
Winter mornings.

Chloe Hopkins (8)
Rangeworthy CE Primary School

WINTER MORNING

Winter morning, winter morning,
I hear the cold breeze,
All the trees start to freeze,
I taste the sparkling white snow,
As the snowman does his show,
I smell the new morn,
As I wait for the dawn,
I see the trees that are bald
And see the misty cold,
I feel the cold ice,
It's smooth, beautiful and nice,
Winter morning, winter morning.

Yasmin Pitman (8)
Rangeworthy CE Primary School

MISTY MORNING

Puddles frozen
Birds singing in the sun
Smooth, slippery ice
Cold face, cold hands
Warm, smoky breath
Light blue sky
Dark blue up above
Crunching leaves.

Katherine Powell (9)
Rangeworthy CE Primary School

WINTER MORNING

Bare trees
Hard grass
The shimmering grass
The glistening frost on the ground
Diamonds of frost
The icy rivers hard and frosty
The colours in the sky
Bare, frosty trees
Icicles hang from roofs
Sparkly windscreens
Smooth, icy puddles.

Kurtis Mastouras (9)
Rangeworthy CE Primary School

A WINTER MORNING

When I woke up, glitter caught my eye
It looked like the stars had fallen from the sky
When I went outside, I saw shimmering diamonds
Glistening on the ground
Bare trees missing their leaves
Birds singing, frost clinging
Crunch, crunch the leaves go as I walk through them

Laura Butler (9)
Rangeworthy CE Primary School

WHAT IF?

What if trees were candyfloss
Or polar bears could fly?
What if the sky was pink
Or if the grass was sugar?

What if rivers were made of honey
Or if fairies danced on the clouds?
What if the world was shaped like a cube
Or if giants roamed in the wood?

What if flowers had faces
Or if goblins lived on the roof?
What if dinosaurs were not extinct
Or if you could catch a falling star?

What if we were 10 foot tall
Or if we were witches and wizards?
What if dragons prowled in caves
Or if ghosts popped in for tea?

What if . . .

Daisy Lindlar (9)
St David's School, Moreton-In-Marsh

NIGHT FEARS

Dark fears,
As the dawn breaks
And the night fades and dies,
Dissolve with shadows into light
And hope.

Carl Hardiman (11)
St David's School, Moreton-In-Marsh

BOYS!

Boys are a pain in the bum
I hear you ask me, 'How come?'
They're nothing but trouble
They'll burst your bubble
And always run home to their mum

Boys are a pain in the neck
I hear you say, 'What the heck!'
But my brother's alright
He is kind and polite
But I think that I better go check

Boys are a pain in the head
You ask, 'What was that you said?'
I've no time for them all
Except maybe Paul
And Johnny and Steven and Fred.

Robyn Thomas (10)
St David's School, Moreton-In-Marsh

WEIRD ANIMALS

Snakes eat lots of cakes,
While elephants bake.
Parrots eat lots of carrots,
While monkeys are in the barracks.
The turtles have just turned purple,
While the dog ate the frog.
Watch out,
The skunk has just turned into a punk.

Esme Baggott (10)
St David's School, Moreton-In-Marsh

MY MAGIC SPOT

Smooth trees brushing in the wind,
Twittering birds singing a lullaby,
Grass calling my name,
With branches dancing with gratitude.

Falling leaves, with trees skipping with the rhythm,
Wet grass tickling my nose and everything,
A touch makes laughter come around me,
Every tree I see makes me sad because my dad left me.

Kieran Evison (11)
St David's School, Moreton-In-Marsh

SEASONS

Summer's often sunny
Spring's when babies are born
Autumn's mostly gloomy
And winter's when it's dark at dawn.

Danielle Tomes (10)
St David's School, Moreton-In-Marsh

ALL ABOUT ME

I'm only 11 and called Adam,
My sister is a proper madam,
She eats a lot
And looks like snot,
So I found her sweets and had 'em!

Daniel Greenwood (9)
St David's School, Moreton-In-Marsh

DISGUSTING JACK

Jack always sucks his toes
Eats his bogey
Asks ugly girls to go out with him

Jack always eats worms
Clean his teeth with mud
Drinks out the fish tank

Jack always eats the house plants
Along with a squished worm
Plus some snot

Jack always sleeps in the dustbin
Munching all the scrap
Then he bites an onion

Last but not least
Puts his head in the toilet!

Mohammed Mifthaul Hassan (10)
St David's School, Moreton-In-Marsh

GREAT NAN

She always smiled,
She always wanted to help,
She offered me glasses of milk
And prepared chocolates and crisps,
I've always loved her,
I still do,
But she's now not here with us,
Or so people say,
But forever in our hearts
And never forgotten.

Samantha Jeffrey (9)
St David's School, Moreton-In-Marsh

BEAUTIFUL FLOWERS

Beautiful flowers
Have wonderful powers
Colourful and smells
Red and bright yellow

Beautiful flowers
Have wonderful powers
Dug in the fresh green grass
As the seeds from flowers pass

Beautiful flowers
Have wonderful powers
Soon they die
On the dark-green grass they lie.

Lucy Jasinski (9)
St David's School, Moreton-In-Marsh

GEORGE MANBY'S LIFE

In the year 1807,
Some men died, some survived,
In the year 1807,
A dozen people died.

In the year 1807,
Sailors went to Heaven,
In the year 1807,
George Manby came along.

In the year 1807,
George Manby had a plan,
In the year 1807,
George Manby, a good man.

Alannah James (9)
St John's CE Primary School, Cheltenham

GEORGE MANBY

This rhyme is about every life
In quite old fashioned days
For stranded sailors no rescue
They died in many ways

Sailors were dying painfully
Nothing was ever done
Everybody hoped gainfully
Until there came the one

Excellent work did he just do
Lots of work of course
To save the lives of stranded crew
Never been done before

Amazing for a cannon so
Also with a strong rope
He was good, he didn't take no
Across the waves sent hope

So off he went to make it work
Over the massive wave
Everyone though he was berserk
No one though he could save

The mortar roars, the rope uncoils
The sailors seize the line
So through the pounding, thrashing sea
So out he came in time

So now they'd found the hero
Now sailors had no fear
Mothers would say cheerio
Knowing sons reappear.

Jessica Morris (9)
St John's CE Primary School, Cheltenham

LIFESAVER - GEORGE MANBY

I watched in terror as they died,
In 1807,
144 lives,
On their way to Heaven.

Until a man called George Manby,
Had a great idea,
He used a cannon and some rope,
George thought and drank rum beer!

He tried and tried, while doing that,
The crew went out to sea.
George succeeded with the cannon,
News came from shipmate Lee.

It was a couple of long days,
On this swaying big ship.
I couldn't help but fear the sea,
I bit and bit my lip.

I thought someone was following,
I looked but no one's there.
Probably just this boring ship
And then I got a scare.

The sky turned black, the winds turned sharp
And then there was a scare.
A shipmate was turned overboard,
His life went through thin air.

I screamed and screamed, it didn't help,
I thought I was dreaming,
George Manby's cannon and the rope,
Came through the air whistling.

The live sailors, including me,
Ran screaming to the rope.
We climbed and climbed, towards the beach
And got given warm cloaks.

So now you know the tale of;
'Lifesaver - George Manby'
He had a very happy life
And lived in proud glory.

Shannon Fairclough (9)
St John's CE Primary School, Cheltenham

THE XYN

(Based on 'The Jabberwocky' by Lewis Carroll)

'Twas brillig in the farftermoon,
Did babbits bounce a bound,
With its eres of flled
And canty of loorb,
Did attack till dead,
Did flide and glide,
Through the trees,
You cannot nur,
You cannot hide,
Xyn has an ofe of scent,
It almost glides over siff,
You cannot neem it,
As it was ment,
'Twas brillig in the farfternoon,
Did babbits bounce a bound.

Jack Davis (10)
St John's CE Primary School, Cheltenham

THE GREAT SUCCESS OF GEORGE MANBY

The destruction of the gun-brig,
Snipe visited Heaven,
She drowned off the coast of Yarmouth,
In 1807.

One hundred and forty-four souls,
Were tossed into the sea,
They died of being cold and drowned,
Manby watched in grief.

He listened to the crew on board,
They were shrieking with death,
Then he had a good idea,
To save the poor men's health.

He toyed with lots of solutions,
He thought and thought – no hope!
When suddenly it came to him:
A cannonball and rope!

The problem was so difficult,
Shooting but not to kill,
He stood upon the sandy shore,
Salt air made him ill.

A murder George Manby would do,
If he did not get this correct,
But he shot it in the right place,
A rowboat out he sent.

One hundred and forty-four men,
Died in the *Snipe* last year,
Seven now luckily survived,
They rowed back without fear.

Manby was so utterly pleased,
In his joy he leapt,
The men came to the sandy beach,
George Manby knelt and wept.

Lucy Bennett (10)
St John's CE Primary School, Cheltenham

GEORGE MANBY'S LIFE

In the year 1807
Some men survived, some died
In the year 1807
Captain Manby saved people's lives

In the year 1807
Manby was a good man
In the year 1807
God they reasoned had sent the storm

In the year 1808
Slowly the rope tightened
In the year 1808
Someone it seemed was still alive

In the year 1808
Once he was confident
In the year 1808
Manby, knelt on the sand and wept

Remember 1808
Remember some men died
Remember 1808
Remember George Manby's brave life.

Chloe Teakle (9)
St John's CE Primary School, Cheltenham

GEORGE MANBY

In the year of 1807,
The wind was a roaring tiger
And the waves were like clouds,
Spreading everywhere.

Captain George Manby,
Thought of something to help,
When he got it,
It was a cannonball tied to a rope.

Captain Manby waited on shore,
Until a ship was wrecked,
But using his cannonball,
A shot correctly and luck came to him.

On the rope there was a pull,
They rushed onto the boat
And rowed as fast as possible,
Back to the shore and hope.

Neekhil Nanawala (9)
St John's CE Primary School, Cheltenham

GEORGE MANBY

In the year 1807,
A big bad storm came,
The ship was tossed from side to side
And one hundred and forty-four lives.

On lots of ships lives were lost,
A gentleman called George,
George Manby was a very clever man,
He worked with sunken ships.

George Manby stopped ships from sinking
And he saved lots of lives,
He made a big fat white balloon
And it goes in a boat.

If the boat is full of water,
It still will float on water.

Amber Dangerfield (10)
St John's CE Primary School, Cheltenham

GISHDEAFAMA
(Based on 'The Jabberwocky' by Lewis Carroll)

'Twas noon and the ribds were ginnis in the odsret
In the onpd the ifsh were miswing
The lilhs were acepulf
The srag was yawswing in the reswin

On the lilhs the Gishdeafama was unchming
On veals off of the Tum Tum tree
Be dink to the Gishdeafama my friends
He is made up of ishf, ragaffe, erde and amal
Be careful of his lacscvas they're archups and olng

He yans and he rowags
He trots and lagops and togles around
The Gishdeafama lives on the lilhs and on the odsret
Friendly is the Gishdeafama

'Twas noon and the ribds were ginnis in the odsret
In the onpd the ifsh were miswing
The lilhs were acepulf
The srag was yaswing in the reswin.

Helen Godding (10)
St John's CE Primary School, Cheltenham

IN 1807

In 1807,
there was a crew,
drowned because of a storm

and today men believe,
that in a storm,
all of the ships will sink,

because of a legend,
people get scared
of sailing out to sea,

A hundred yards from shore,
Manby watched ships
sink beneath sharp rocks.

A pirate did all this,
Ralph the Rover,
he's done it lots of times.

A rock with a big hole,
sank many ships,
day and night, day and night,

so never go out there,
for fear of death
and never be seen again.

Miranda Howard (10)
St John's CE Primary School, Cheltenham

CAPTAIN GEORGE MANBY

In the year 1807,
Sailors risked their lives,
They tried to survive the deep sea,
But didn't succeed.

The hurling and buffeting wind,
That one stormy night,
It whipped them away and killed them,
That one windy night.

Several early versions failed,
While crew was at sea,
They took a visit to Heaven
And slowly sank to their knees.

They needed to live their own lives,
To see their loved ones,
They comforted out at sea,
To see their young sons.

Now meet the captain of the ship,
Captain George Manby,
He makes sure we don't go too far,
Out into the sea.

They had safe journeys in the sea,
Manby saved their lives,
He rescued some seven people,
By his magic motor lifeline.

Hazelanne Abbott (9)
St John's CE Primary School, Cheltenham

RAMEL
(Based on 'The Jabberwocky' by Lewis Carroll)

'Twas nevning and thi sosasis was still and clear
And thi malm eert had going cocotuns.
Lives by sosasis in thi tersed
And the snacrocs ate their tuns

It has humpy kab stumpy gels,
Going tointy reas
And long long shishkers that flickers flies
And a little fluff fluff

It movs very soly
An snorts when stared at
Ramel is verry friendly
And friendly with other great manchures

It eats prickly stick
And different sorts of plants
Shelpy teeth teeth
An long claws

'Twas nevning and thi sosasis was still and clear
And thi malmeert had going cocotuns
Lives by sosasis in thi
And the snacrocs ate their tuns.

Candice Holland (10)
St John's CE Primary School, Cheltenham

THE SPICOARK
(Based on 'The Jabberwocky' by Lewis Carroll)

'Twas moonpam in the wibley,
The platres flyky in the carbox,
All the mallins ushing to the wariter,
In the platres birds were gining.

Beware the spico my son!
Claws that catch, a tail that scratches,
I gilufs the tafs, the tafs of the malins
And slifs them on the platres.

It glums like a tiges,
Stuffing in the wibley like a beley
And slings in the wariter slufly
And spico not a sloby mallin.

It hides on the platrress
And cleepy finds some mallin,
Swiks from the platress
And gilufs it and sleeks.

'Twas noonpam in the wibley,
The platres flyky in the carbox,
All the mallins whing to the wariter,
In the platres birds were gining.

Denis Thomas (11)
St John's CE Primary School, Cheltenham

THE WHIRLPOOL

The whirlpool is a tornado destroying
everything in its path

It is a blue spiral
pushed downs to the ocean floor

It is a blue sky
that God watches us

It is the blue
That shines in your eye

It is a blue whirlpool
the fearsome destroyer.

Curtis Phillips (11)
St John's CE Primary School, Coleford

WHAT IS . . . THE SWIMMING POOL?

The swimming pool is an army of people
Who just had a water fight

It is a moving blue rectangle
Seen from the sky

It is a sea
Waiting to be swum in

It is a village
That people have always shared

It is a sheet of blue paper
With the smell of chlorine.

Leighann James (10)
St John's CE Primary School, Coleford

BARBECUE

Sausages sizzling
Burgers baking
Chicken's cooking
Sisters serving

Dads drinking
Babies bathing
Dogs digging
Brothers bothering

Mums moaning
Aunties annoying
Cats clawing
What a day!

Richard Wagstaff (10)
St John's CE Primary School, Coleford

WHAT IS ... THE STREAM?

The stream is a piece of rope
Winding along

It is a long snake
Slithering through the grass

It is a snail's trail
Sliding down the path

It is a horse's tail
Swishing away the flies

It is a bird
Flying down to its prey.

Laura Dymond (10)
St John's CE Primary School, Coleford

THE DREAM

Dream away, sleepyhead
Go to bed, go to bed
Lie head on pillow
Go to bed, go to bed
Pull the covers up
Goodnight

Whirl away
What's your dream
My dream house and garden
No! The fields far away
Help me make a dream

Tell me something, not a horror
A dream, oh yes let's dream about that

Ah, I can hear the wind, the birds, flowers, butterflies
I can feel the wind, sun and nature
Oh, it's a dream!

Beep! Beep!
Holler, it's gone
Help, time to go to school
No!

Sophie Alexander (11)
St John's CE Primary School, Coleford

WHAT IS . . . THE OCEAN?

The ocean is God's bath, tears of God,
It is a roaring machine that cannot stop,
It is made to be seen.

Derry Burge (11)
St John's CE Primary School, Coleford

WHAT IS . . . A CLOUD?

A cloud is candyfloss
Flying in the air

It is a fluffy pillow
On a big blue bed

It is cotton wool
Floating in a swimming pool.

Joseph Bovill-Baker (10)
St John's CE Primary School, Coleford

HULLABALOO

I've got to write a poem,
I don't know what to do.
My teacher says
It's got to be
About this hullabaloo.

I'm sitting with my biro,
It hovers above the page,
Waiting for inspiration, it seems such an age.

Everyone else is writing,
'Oh what, oh what shall I do?'
I can't think of anything
That rhymes with hullabaloo.

I've got to write this poem,
No matter what I do
And all I can think of writing,
Is hullabaloo, hullabaloo, hullabaloo.

Laurie Joseph Miller (10)
St Lawrence Primary School, Lechlade

MY DREAM

I've had a dream since I was eleven
To be the famous 007
To shoot the baddies with my gun
To drive my car and make them run
To win the reward and be a hero
To put the evil ones in jail so they have zero
This has been my dream since I was eleven
Someday I'll be the famous 007.

George Somers (10)
St Lawrence Primary School, Lechlade

GARDENS

G   reen crops in the meadows
A   fresh batch of golden corn
R   ich flowers in the fruitful garden
D   ays, summer days, playing in the garden
E   nding days looking at the sunset
N   ow we all go to bed
S   unset and the day is finally gone.

Laura Griffiths (11)
St Lawrence Primary School, Lechlade

BY THE CURTAINS

By the curtains I can see
The darkness
Of a shadow
The shadow has
Long, stretching fingers
With a nose pointing straight at me

I step into the darkness
But all I can see
Is no stretching fingers
And no pointing nose
Just plain old me!

Olivia Sharpe (11)
St Lawrence Primary School, Lechlade

ME

I've got a hobby playing with my friends,
I've got two pets, Chocolate and Fudge
I've got a bike, it's orange and white,
I've got some friends, Megan and Lizzie,
I've got a brother he's called Nick,
I've got a family, they're just great,
I've got a garden, it's covered with grass,
I've got a den, it's dark and grey,
I'm so lucky, I've got so much.

Jessica Bennett (10)
St Lawrence Primary School, Lechlade

SPIDERS

Spiders are hairy!
Spiders are scary!
Spiders are small,
Sometimes they crawl,
They scare the dogs
When they hide under logs.

Scary, hairy spiders!

Ollie Williams (10)
St Lawrence Primary School, Lechlade

THE ROLLER COASTER

The roller coaster goes up and down,
My head is spinning round and round,
The wind rushes by, really quick,
I feel like I'm gonna be sick.

The thrust of the ride,
Nearly throws me off the side,
Up comes the dip
And my head starts to tip.

I feel like I'm flying
And even though I'm trying,
I'm gonna puke,
All over my brother, Luke.

Danny Lee (10)
St Lawrence Primary School, Lechlade

BOOKS

I flicked my page to read next,
My brain is full of fantasy,
I heard my heart beat like a drum,
My eyes were full of words.
I leaned to my book to see more close,
Someone was calling me, but I didn't notice,
What will happen next?
My brain is just full of that.

I read on more,
He's saved!
I finally got my breath back
And rested my tired eyes.

Risa Oka (11)
St Lawrence Primary School, Lechlade

SCARED

When I tiptoe out my bedroom in the middle of the night
I hear the floorboards creaking, it gives me an awful fright

I run back in and hop into bed
And pull the covers right over my head

I slowly pull them off again and peep out of one eye
But all I can see is the pitch-black like the midnight sky

I can't help but think, what could be there?
I have a funny feeling it's flowing through the air

I wake up in the morning and hear the birds up high
I open up my curtains and say, 'How lucky am I?'

Gabby Rieunier (11)
St Lawrence Primary School, Lechlade

MY SECRET

I have a secret nobody knows,
Inside me it just grows and grows.
I'm not sure if it's good or bad,
But I know it will make someone glad.

The secret inside me twists and turns
And every day it burns and burns.
The secret inside me, it hurts so bad,
It drives me crazy and makes me mad.

The secret inside me, it tries to get out,
It wibbles and wobbles just like a trout.
What would you do if you had a secret like mine?
It would make you shiver right down your spine.

Zoë Leonard (11)
St Lawrence Primary School, Lechlade

THE POWER OF A SECRET

Secrets are dangerous things,
They cause evil desires and dark thoughts,
They hide in their depths of concealment,
They cause danger,
They are conquerors of people,
They create diseases of the mind,
A secret holds a power far greater than any being,
It is the breaker of hearts,
The ruler of souls.

Luke Jackson-Ross (11)
St Lawrence Primary School, Lechlade

FOOTBALL

F   ootball is great
O   ver the ground they run
O   ver the goalie, the ball goes in
T   he crowd cheers
B   eckham does his celebration
A   nd the manager is pleased
L   ucky Beckham does his manager proud
L   ittle Brooklyn is proud as his dad makes him happy.

Kieran New (10)
St Lawrence Primary School, Lechlade

MY DREAM

I had a dream that I was fifteen
I was big, strong and very mean
I was bigger than a monster who is green
I had a dream that I was fifteen
I had a dream that I was fifteen
I started a food fight with a bean

The messiest fight you've ever seen
I had a dream that I was fifteen
I had a dream that I was fifteen
I belonged to a football team
I was so brilliant the crowd screamed
In my dream.

James White (11)
St Lawrence Primary School, Lechlade

HULLABALOO

I have a dog called little Jay
I don't know what to do
I took him for a walk one day
And he made a hullabaloo

In a field there is a large cow
She makes a whining moo
My dad says that he'll fix her now
And she sings a hullabaloo

I also have a cream canary
He's as bad as the rest of the crew
He looks as sweet as a fairy
But makes a hullabaloo

In my garden lives a tiny toad
It's as bad as the others too
When it switches into singing mode
It makes a hullabaloo

But my guinea pig is worst of all
She does nothing but chew
Her gnawing drives me up the wall
She makes a hullabaloo.

Peter Lee (10)
St Lawrence Primary School, Lechlade

MY UN-NORMAL FAMILY

My family isn't normal,
There is always a row in the house.
My brother eats anything at all
And my sister tortures her mouse.

My mum drops a china plate,
Almost every day,
My dad needs a haircut,
His hair looks like a bundle of hay.

The only normal person in my family,
It has to be me,
I think I'm the only one,
There is no 'we'.

Alice Brookes (10)
St Lawrence Primary School, Lechlade

SWIMMING

Playing in the water, playing with my friend,
Splish, splash in the pool,
Swim, swim, I'm going under,
Kick, splash, kick, splash, I am under the water,
Drowning, blowing bubbles,
Slowly slipping down the side of the pool to the bottom,
Waving my arms fast, trying to catch someone's attention,
All of a sudden I feel something touching me,
I am so lucky that someone has found me.

Lucy Bailey (10)
St Lawrence Primary School, Lechlade

THE BOMB

Once a bomb was built
In New York City
Then it got blown up
And it was such a pity
Thirty people died
And some survived
Their families were sad
And others were mad
The bomb recovered
They rebuilt it again
And tried it once more
It blew up the bank
Now the families are very, very poor.

Harry Bennett (8)
St Paul's CE Primary School, Gloucester

NUMBER NONSENSE

One old optimistic octopus,
Two tale-telling tangerines,
Three thick, thorny thieves,
Four forfeiting flamingos,
Five fire flirting fellas,
Six slimy, sly snakes,
Seven suspicious sisters,
Eight evil elephants,
Nine nasty, naughty newts,
Ten bad-tempered toucans.

Kaitlyn Brokenshire (8)
St Paul's CE Primary School, Gloucester

RUN QUICK!

Quick, run fast the sweet shop is closing.
Quick, run fast the school is closing.
Quick, run fast the market is closing.
Quick, run fast the library is closing.

Quick, run fast or the swings in the park will be gone.
Quick, run fast or the crisps will be gone.
Quick, run fast or the chocolate will be gone.
Quick, run fast or the biscuits will be gone.

Quick, run fast and go home or the door will be closed.
Bang! Bang! Bang!

Bhavisha Gajjar (9)
St Paul's CE Primary School, Gloucester

TEN THINGS FOUND IN A SECRET BOX

One microscopic crumb
Two bits of nail from my thumb
Three shiny rings
Four dead ducks that used to quack
Five old matches
Six broken latches
Seven smashed plates
Eight rusted gates,
Nine smelly socks,
Ten over-wound clocks.

James Beaumont (9)
St Paul's CE Primary School, Gloucester

LIGHTNING!

Thundery fingers come crushing down
Trashing the air with a piercing sound
Like a fork stabbing its prey, flashing bright it shines so brightly,
It lights the night
Like a white blanket blocking the sky
Shivering and shattering way up high
Like a clap in the air
The thunder screeches its moaning sound
Like a thunder bird clapping its dazzling wings
It flies away for the rest of the day
As it sings its snappy song.

William Barker (9)
St Paul's CE Primary School, Gloucester

CREATURES OF THE SEA

Under the waves so big and blue
Live fantastic creatures that will amaze you!
Like the squidgy octopus with long tentacle legs
And the hard-shelled oyster that lays millions of eggs
There are fish that can fly above the waves
And fierce-looking eels that lurk deep in caves
So make sure you look carefully before entering the sea
I don't want a shark's teeth to bite you or me!

Paul D'Alquen (9)
St Paul's CE Primary School, Gloucester

BEST FRIENDS

My friends
My best friends
Friends play and laugh
And say, 'Let's play!'
Friends go around friends'
Houses to play
And friends go places together
And friends do what they
Think they should do
Best friends go bike riding
Up ramps

Best friends sleep over their friend's house
They play on the streets
Best friends stick together!

Jamie Bishop (9)
St Paul's CE Primary School, Gloucester

THE SCHOOL DINNERS

Slugs in the cabbage
The out-of-date chips
The mouldy bananas
The rotten cheese dips
The dirty orange skin, covered in pips
The cabbage was smelly.

Can you pick?

Evangeline Young (8)
St Paul's CE Primary School, Gloucester

THE CREEPY CASTLE

Go inside the creepy castle
And see what's inside
Lurking about is a goblin
Saying, 'Please be my friend.'

Go inside the creepy castle
And see what's inside
Hovering about like crazy
Down the spooky hall
Is a ghost saying, 'I'm doomed.'

Go inside the creepy castle
And see what's inside
Sneaking about in the smelly cellar
Is a zombie saying, 'I'm losing my bones.'

Go inside the creepy castle
And see what's inside
Jumping up and down is a mummy
Screaming, 'Argh!'

Go inside the creepy castle
And see what's inside
Waiting for you is a goblin
Ghost, zombie, mummy and a vampire

It's horror!

Michael Carpenter (9)
St Paul's CE Primary School, Gloucester

THE BEST THINGS IN LIFE

My favourite colour is *blue*
My favourite thing to do
I love going swimming
In the deep *blue* sea

My favourite food is *ice cream*
So yummy, yum, yum, yum
Whenever I see it
I think of my tummy, tum, tum

My favourite *friends*
Are Dieter who is very funny
Evie who acts like a little bunny
Bhavisha who does whatever she should
And Rahima who is very good

My favourite *animal*
Is the slinky cat
Who has great big eyes
I think it could win a prize
For the way it moves
Its fur is so silky and smooth.

Poppy Norton (9)
St Paul's CE Primary School, Gloucester

THE MAGIC GENIE

I found a magic genie
And I asked for 3 wishes

I asked the genie for my first wish
And I said, 'Can I have all the chocolate in the world?'

I asked the genie for my second wish
And I said, 'Can you give me a million pounds?'

I asked the genie for my last wish
And I said, 'Can you turn me into a wizard?'

George Bailey (9)
St Paul's CE Primary School, Gloucester

DON'T DO THAT!

Don't do, don't do that
Don't pull faces
Don't be rude at school
Don't tease the cat
Who do they think I am
Some kind of fool?

Don't pick your nose
Don't kick
Who do they think I am
Sam rat?

One day they will say
Don't throw fruit at the computer
Do what?
Don't throw fruit at the computer

Don't rip the book
Don't play up
Don't beat up kids!

Don't do that because . . .
You are the teacher!

Dieter Douglas (8)
St Paul's CE Primary School, Gloucester

TRAINS

T   rains are very fast, *chou, chou,*
R   ails are for the trains, *tratal, tratal, tratal,*
A   train is a machine, a machine,
I   think trains are good, good, good, good,
N   ails in the track go *ratar, ratar, ratar.*

Lewis Hood (9)
St Paul's CE Primary School, Gloucester

O RAFFLES

O Raffles, what big brown eyes you have,
Your mane flies in the wind,
How shiny and silky your coat is
As I stroke my hand over it,
Your thin tail gets knotted up in the straw,
But I don't mind because I love brushing you!
O Raffles, o Raffles, you are my best friend.

Rebecca Berry (11)
Sherborne CE Primary School

THE SANDPIPER

He races at the sea with a blunder,
Waits for the waves as they crash like thunder,
He races around looking for food
As he jollies about in his lashing mood,
He's looking for food as he scurries around,
He hits a rock and tumbles to the ground,
The sea scoops him up from the shore,
Then he awakens and comes back for more.

Eloise Farrow (11)
Sherborne CE Primary School

FIRE

Fire, you're the best
People say you're mischief
But I don't think so
You jump like big horses
Let alone you're only a little pony
Let's go on a ride
Gallop along the downs
Canter through the rivers
I love you flamey Fire.

Hannah Berry (11)
Sherborne CE Primary School

WHAT'S FOR TEA?

What's for tea?
English sounds good
Chips and beans
I'd rather have pud

What's for tea?
French never fails
Urgh! Disgusting
Boiled snails

What's for tea?
Indian in a hurry
Um! Red peppers
What about the curry?

What's for tea?
Spinach
Urgh! I'm not eating that!

Luke Stranks (11)
Siddington CE Primary School

A MONSTER

A monster,
A monster under your bed
Coming . . .
To get *you!*

Don't be scared
It might be friendly
It might be scary
But if it is friendly, don't cry
If it is scary, cry, cry loudly
So your mum and dad can wake up
And kill it quickly
So you can get some sleep.

Emily Kilby (9)
Siddington CE Primary School

A FANCY DRESS PARTY

Go to the party dressed as an orc,
Scare all the people while they talk!
Go to the party dressed like a tree,
Boy, oh boy, I hope those bees don't sting me.
Go to the party dressed like a horse,
Oh no! Here comes that mouse.
Go to the party dressed like a boat,
Oh no! I forgot how to float.
Go to the party dressed like a chair,
Here comes a blind man called Bo-tare!

Thomas Porter (10)
Siddington CE Primary School

SOARING PLANES

Planes,
Soaring planes high
Above in the sky.

Planes,
Their wings are like an ice cream cone
And their rudders are like big, fast fans.

Planes,
Their wheels are like liquorice
And their windows are like fish tanks.

Planes,
Their cockpits are like a big arcade.

Planes,
Soaring planes,
In the air.

Luke Moore (10)
Siddington CE Primary School

MY MOTHER

Mess-hater,
Silence-breaker,
Book-reader,
Child-feeder,
Soap-watcher

Baby-adorer
Children-lover

That's my mother.

Letisha Jessop (9)
Siddington CE Primary School

A SPOOKY FANCY DRESS PARTY

A fancy dress party,
Come as a witch,
With a big, pointy hat,
Which witch is which?

A fancy dress party,
Come as a cat,
With a long, black tail,
Fancy that.

A fancy dress party,
Come as a wizard,
Turn water into Coke
And a dog to a lizard.

A fancy dress party,
Come as a dragon,
Don't burn down the hall
Or my little toy wagon.

A fancy dress party,
Come as a bat,
Eat all the mice,
But not my pet rat.

A fancy dress party,
Come as a teacher,
Did you see the film Scream?
He was the main feature.

Amber Jane Stranks (11)
Siddington CE Primary School

A FANCY DRESS PARTY

A fancy dress party,
Come as a pop star,
Singing and dancing,
But no posh car.

A fancy dress party,
Come as a football star,
Shorts and a T-shirt,
Didn't come far.

A fancy dress party,
Come as a clown,
Big, orange hair
And a small, stripy gown.

A fancy dress party,
Come as a cat,
Whiskers and a tail,
No one thought of that.

A fancy dress party,
Come as a bear,
Big and bushy,
Lots of hair.

A fancy dress party,
Come as a dog,
Small and brown
And fat as a log.

What will you come as?

Danielle Walker (11)
Siddington CE Primary School

WHAT'S FOR TEA?

What's for tea
I like toast
By the coast
I eat bananas
In pyjamas
I wish for
A cake by
The lake
I would
Love my
Tea by
The sea
Now I wonder, what's for tea?

Emma Reeve (11)
Siddington CE Primary School

MY BROTHER

He hogs the TV
He hogs the PS2
He eats my chocolate
He reads my book
He rips up my homework
He's annoying
Guess who he is?
My big brother.

Edward Nellist (10)
Siddington CE Primary School

WISHES

Wishes go wrong
Wishes come true
Wishes come from a genie that you never, ever knew
Wishes are magic
Wishes are unexplainable
Wishing stars
Have you seen them all?

Laura May Smith (10)
Siddington CE Primary School

NIGHT-TIME

Owls go tu-whit tu-whoo in the night,
Bats fly in the sky,
Foxes look for things to eat,
Badgers' eyes glow in the moonlight,
Hedgehogs roll in the road
And that's what happens in the night.

Ben Hughes (11)
Temple Guiting CE Primary School

FROM A CAT'S EYES

From a cat's eyes the world looks like a . . .
Climbing frame towering up to the sky or a curtain hanging so high,
From a dog's eyes the world looks like . . .
Black and white whilst it is never light,
From a race horse's eyes the world looks like a . . .
Sandy long gallop or a bronze and a carrot,
But from my eyes the world looks like a giant *quiz!*

Camilla Lee-Warner (10)
Temple Guiting CE Primary School

PUSSY CAT

Pussy, pussy, pussy cat, sitting on the wall
Pussy, pussy, pussy cat, waiting for his call
Pussy, pussy, pussy cat, glitter and glamour
Pussy, pussy, pussy cat, making lots of clamour

Pussy, pussy, pussy cat, always cleaning her paws
Pussy, pussy, pussy cat, always making her own laws
Pussy, pussy, pussy cat, always in a dream
Pussy, pussy, pussy cat, she always looks like she's got the cream.

Ana Coelho (9)
Temple Guiting CE Primary School

THE GOLDEN EAGLE

The golden eagle in the breeze,
Floating in mid-air,
Down he pounces on a mouse,
As quick as lightning,
Bolt, off he goes back to base,
With a mouse for the family,
In the nest,
The young eagles grow big and strong,
So they can catch their own prey,
In the wide open world.

Tim Sheasby (11)
Temple Guiting CE Primary School

GOING TO THE BEACH

I'm going to the beach today,
Would you like to come?
I'll take my ball to play,
Only if you'll stay.

I'm going surfing in the sea,
Would you like to come?
You can come and practice with me
And then we will be free.

We have finished at the sea,
The orange sun has gone down.
We had such a lovely time, you see,
Having to go home now – we frown!

Christopher Hughes (10)
Temple Guiting CE Primary School

THE BEST GRANNY EVER!

My granny is a sofa that you sink in to and a deep blue colour.
My granny is a silken poppy swaying in the breeze.
My granny is an old English sheepdog, sweet and plods on the beach.
My granny is a big duvet, always around to have a cuddle.
My granny is as cool as a cucumber.
My granny is the *best granny ever!*

Isabelle Mangan (10)
Temple Guiting CE Primary School

THE STRANGE OLD MAN AND HIS PARROT, NED

A strange old man walked down the street
Looking for some food to eat

The strange old man found a comfy seat
It was very tidy and very neat

The strange old man was having fun
While he was eating a sticky bun

The strange old man got up from his chair
While doing the cancan with a bear

The strange old man went to bed
'I'm real tired,' said his pet parrot, Ned, who had a big head

Which he couldn't fit into bed, so he had to go in the shed
Made out of lead, which was painted red, as a warning for Ned
Not to lick the lead.
But he did instead and the strange old man said,
'Poor Ned . . . he's dead!'

Gregory Muskett (11)
Temple Guiting CE Primary School

LIMERICK

There once was a man from Peking,
Who always went *ding, ding, ding!*
He swallowed a bell,
That tasted real swell
And then he began to swing.

Emily Spurling (9)
Temple Guiting CE Primary School

THE JUNGLE

Lions prowling for their prey,
Then a tiger saves the day.

Parrots flying really low,
Looking like a colourful rainbow.

All the rhinos in a stampede,
Surging forward at a great speed.

Hyenas laughing in the sun,
Dancing around, having fun.

Monkeys swinging from tree to tree,
Oh, I'd love to be that free.

Now I've seen what's in the jungle,
My brain has got into a bungle.

James Boote (10)
Temple Guiting CE Primary School

ANIMALS

Monkeys swinging from tree to tree
Careful where you land, there is a chimpanzee

Parrots squawking in the trees
Their feathers fluttering in the breeze

Crocs crawling in the swamp
Looking for something to chomp

Snakes slithering on the ground
I would give anything not to hear another sound.

Matthew Shelley (9)
Temple Guiting CE Primary School

CHESS

The queen appears before you,
You fear her more than the rest,
The blacks will soon have victory,
Menacing in every way.

Your knight calls out, 'Check,'
To be pounced on by the queen.
She spares not a soul that moves to protect,
She makes a clear path and then checkmate!

You will not give in,
You have strength yet.
Your knight moves quickly to affect,
We have victory!

Eleanor Thornett (10)
Temple Guiting CE Primary School

SURFERS

The waves are high
The waves are dangerous
There is a red flag
Just right for the surfers
Their necklaces gleam in the sun
Now they're having great fun
They climb up onto their boards
They hit the waves with a splash.

Matthew Houldsworth (10)
Temple Guiting CE Primary School

ANIMAL ANTICS

Mice are running on the floor
Something jumps out, there is a roar
Penguins wobbling out of their hut
They break the ice and get a cut
Ponies running through the field
I hope that the farm gate is sealed
Eagles swooping in the air
Homing in on somebody's lair
Little fishes in the deep blue ocean
Somebody on the beach drops their lotion.

Sam Twiston Davies (10)
Temple Guiting CE Primary School

LIONS

Lions prowl at night
Looking for a fight
They don't find one
So they carry on

Eventually they find their prey
Go for that one, is what they say
They start to prowl
While hyenas howl . . .

The morning is near
The prey isn't here
Now they retreat
Their stomachs full of meat.

Michael Carthew (10)
Temple Guiting CE Primary School

OWL

Loud hooter
Not a tooter

Rodent picker
Not a licker

Night flyer
Higher and higher

Good lander
Getting grander

What is it?

An owl!

Sophie Chambers (10)
Temple Guiting CE Primary School

POSH

She's a poodle lying on a claret cushion,
A high-pitched voice,
With an annoyed tone,
Always wanting to be pampered,
Always showing off,
She always wants what is best,
She only chooses the best,
She only chooses the most expensive
And won't go for anything less.

Joanna Porter (9)
Temple Guiting CE Primary School

ANIMALS

One wonderful, whistling worm,
Two toy tigers taking toy tweezers,
Three tall thugs thistling thin things,
Four fighting fans fishing for fish.

Five fat flowers fighting thugs,
Six sickly snakes slithering in snot,
Seven silly slugs sliming snakes,
Eight enormous elephants eating echoey eggs,
Nine naughty nits nibbling Nike knickers,
Ten terrible, ticklish trees trying to tell tales about a tiger.

Sophie Turner (7)
Winchcombe Abbey CE Primary School

PUPPIES

Little, happy, mischievous pups,
Rolling round on their little backs,
Under the shady tree.

Little, happy, mischievous pups,
Digging up Mum's flower beds,
Playing happily in the garden.

Little, lively, playful pups,
Chewing the grass,
Under their mother's guard.

Ricola Mitchell (7)
Winchcombe Abbey CE Primary School

IF YOU REALLY, REALLY WANT TO SEE A MONKEY...

If you really want to see a monkey,
You must go down to the creepy, sleepy jungle,
I know a monkey living there,
He's a cool, he's a cheeky, he's a freaky monkey
Yes, if you really want to go down to the creepy, sleepy jungle,
Go down and say, 'Monkey, wonky, chunky monkey,'
And up she'll pop,
Don't stick around, run for your life!

Tessa Warby (7)
Winchcombe Abbey CE Primary School

MY FRIEND AND ME

My friend came to play the other day,
She has long, blonde hair,
She has high-heels, they are red,
She said, 'Hello.'
I said, 'Come in, come in.'
I said, 'Come and play in my bedroom.'
We played and played, then we had tea,
The next day we tidied my bedroom.

Lucy Newsum (7)
Winchcombe Abbey CE Primary School

MY ROOM IS MESSY

My room is messy, as messy as can be,
Filled with toys and all kinds of things,
But it's not me, it's my brother!
He's a naughty boy, as naughty as can be!

My room is tidy, as tidy as can be,
All the toys are packed away,
But it's not me, it's my brother!
He's a good boy, as good as can be.

Harry Scammell (7)
Winchcombe Abbey CE Primary School

STARS

Glittering, shimmering, shining stars,
Shining out so bright,
Shimmering and shining above Mars,
But only for one night.

Soon the stars go back
And meanwhile the day begins,
Soon the day's not black
And you would not see the moon.

Leah Lane (7)
Winchcombe Abbey CE Primary School

MY PET

My pet is a pest,
My pet is sweet at times,
My pet loves his toys,
My pet loves his food!
My pet loves choosing things,
My pet hates baths,
My pet likes to hide.

Lucy Clarke (7)
Winchcombe Abbey CE Primary School